Living Boldly

Other titles by Phyllis Hobe

When Love Isn't Easy
Never Alone

Phyllis Hobe

Living Boldly

COLLIER BOOKS
Macmillan Publishing Company
New York

To Judy Mead

*whose courage has helped so many of us
to live a little more boldly*

Collier Books
Macmillan Publishing Company
866 Third Avenue, New York, N.Y. 10022
Collier Macmillan Canada, Inc.

Library of Congress Cataloging-in-Publication Data
Hobe, Phyllis.
Living boldly / Phyllis Hobe.
p.   cm.
ISBN 0-02-033271-8
1. Christian life—1960-   2. Hobe, Phyllis.   I. Title.
BV4501.2.H5313   1989   89-7355   CIP
248.4—dc20

Macmillan books are available at special discounts for bulk purchases for
sales promotions, premiums, fund-raising, or education use.
For details, contact:
Special Sales Director
Macmillan Publishing Company
866 Third Avenue
New York, N.Y. 10022

10 9 8 7 6 5 4 3 2 1

Printed in the United States of America

Contents

ꝫ

Contents

Preface

————————— ❧ —————————

THERE IS SOMETHING IN me that I can call on for help when I cannot help myself—and that is God. I'm only sorry it took me so long to realize that He is not out there, but in here.

Let me give you an example.

Some years ago a friend asked me to write the copy for a brochure advertising a small country inn that he and his wife had bought. I said no, I couldn't.

"But you're a writer!" he protested. "Writers can write anything."

"No," I said, laughing. "Writing ads is one thing—books are something else. You need a specialist."

Well, you know how it goes: he's your friend and he needs help. He believes in you—and he doesn't know any other writers. So you say yes—if you're as foolish as I was.

I ended up doing a lot of things I didn't know how to do—choosing color photographs, asking another friend to design the layout, arranging with a printer to produce what had become a very handsome piece of work. "This is running into money," I kept telling my friend. And he kept telling me not to worry. Just send him the bills. I knew he could afford to pay them, yet he didn't. The photographer, the printer, and the designer were understanding of my predicament, but the fact remained that they had to be paid—and I was the one who had placed the orders.

It's very hard to get tough with a friend. I had lunch with him, I sent him letters and copies of the bills, I telephoned. And he kept telling me he would take care of everything. Finally it became clear that he wouldn't, and that I had to. But I didn't know how.

By no means did I have the money to pay for such an extravagant project. I was also intimidated by my friend; he was so certain that he had done nothing wrong. What would he think of me if I took him to court? I would lose a friend. I would also be involved in a costly long-term legal battle.

It was time to ask God for help, which of course I did. And I assumed that help would come in the form of something tangible: my friend would have a change of heart and run for his checkbook; our creditors would wait for payment indefinitely; I would have a windfall and use some of it to pay the accounts. I believed that these were the sort of things God could do.

When absolutely nothing happened, I called my lawyer. "Look," he said, "this is no big deal. You don't even have to bring me into it." He told me to go to the District Judge and file a claim against my friend. It was an inexpensive process. "Spend a few extra dollars and have a sheriff deliver the summons," my lawyer instructed me. This was hardball we were playing, and I wasn't sure I was ready for it. Frankly, I was scared. While I wanted to keep my friend for a friend, I certainly didn't want him for an enemy. He was a lot tougher than I was.

"Lord, give me courage," I prayed.

I waited a few more days, and nothing happened. That is, nothing picked me up and delivered me to the District Judge's office. Then I realized that God had already given me courage—and I had to do something with it. To make a long story short, I filled out the proper forms and arranged to have the summons delivered by a sheriff, which shook my friend up enough to convince him that I meant business. The bills were paid, I did lose a friend, but I learned a few things from the experience.

Most important is that God doesn't remove our problems—He teaches us how to deal with them. And when we ask Him for help, we have to be willing to do something with the help He gives us.

God has always been close to me, although I haven't always thought of Him in that sense. For much of my life I thought of Him as Someone to call on in emergencies, and I tried not to have any. Of course, I didn't succeed. I failed as many times as you did, possibly more. I made some wrong decisions and stuck to them because I didn't want to admit they were wrong. Sometimes I expected more out of life than I could get. On the other hand, I didn't always try hard enough to get what I wanted.

I never went to God at the beginning of anything. I always went to Him last, when everything I tried to do was falling apart. He was my Rescuer. I didn't mean to slight Him, and I never hesitated to go to Him when I was desperate. I just didn't think I had the right to bother Him with anything that wasn't urgent. After all, there are a lot of other people and a lot of other problems in the world.

He never let me down. He didn't always provide the answer I was seeking—sometimes He came up with a better one. He never made my problems go away, but He walked through them with me, and very often I came out of them with something valuable that I was able to use later in my life. Not once did He remind me that I had brought my troubles on myself. Not once did He ask me for anything in return for all He did for me.

Always I came away with my arms loaded with blessings—and a tremendous sense of indebtedness. How could I possibly repay Him? I hadn't earned His gifts. What must He think of me for being so needy? So many of my prayers began with something like, "Forgive me, Lord, for asking You again, but. . . ." I lived for the day when I could stop bothering Him and take care of myself. And yet I know now that the one thing He wanted of me was to call on Him more often. Constantly, in fact.

I would have, except that I just didn't know any better. I loved God very much, but all I knew about love was the way I felt about other people and the way they felt about me. There was only so much we could give to each other without taking away from ourselves, so we were careful of our love. There had to be enough to go around. You didn't ask for more—or for any, sometimes—unless you had a good reason. That was the way I thought God loved. If you needed Him, you didn't go to Him until you had used up all your own strength and all you could get from anyone else. You didn't want to be pushy.

But there were times when I felt God's presence in my life for no particular reason, and they were special to me. Such as the summer vacations I spent with my parents at a mountain lake in New Jersey, when I would get up very early so I could see the sun rise and flicker on the water—before that peaceful reflection was jigsaw-puzzled by speedboats, water skiers, swimmers, and the happy sound of children, I among them. I was always the first one up, and I moved quietly so I wouldn't disturb my parents. I'd go down to the dock, get into the rowboat, and glide silently halfway across the lake. As the sun came up over the night-darkened hillsides, I'd ship the oars and just float. To me it was more than beautiful. I felt as if I were sitting in on a miracle—the beginning of a new day—and I enjoyed being in the presence of God without having to ask Him for anything. I never considered that He might have enjoyed having me there, too.

I also remember the long bus trips I used to take to visit my mother in the hospital the winter I was twelve. I was afraid I was going to lose my mother, and I had prayed fervently for her recovery from a serious operation. And she *was* improving. But it would be a long time before she could come home, and so, every afternoon after school, I went to see her. I'd wave good-bye to my friends at school and watch them go in the other direction while I waited on the corner for the bus. I felt very lonely seeing them going toward home. Probably their mothers were waiting for them, or maybe they'd be home for dinner. And my mother—well, we weren't sure yet.

I felt God's presence on every one of those bus trips. It didn't matter how many other people there were, or whether anyone was sitting next to me. He was always closer. I felt a bit guilty because I hadn't asked for His company, and maybe someone else needed God's attention more than I did, but I was glad He was there. He made the loneliness go away.

As I grew up, there were fewer of those special moments, perhaps because I was too busy with other things—trying to make something of myself, trying to make other people happy, trying to make sense out of life. I got in touch with God often because I had a lot of emergencies, and, as always, He came to my aid. But somehow that wasn't enough. I wanted more—of what, I didn't know. I only knew that the harder I tried to do what I thought was right, the more things went wrong. I was ashamed to need God as much as I did. Yet I almost welcomed the crises that brought me to Him.

I didn't tell Him how empty my life was, because I didn't think anything could be done about it. I had worked very hard, but I didn't enjoy what I did. I knew what I wanted to do, but I was afraid I wouldn't succeed. Besides, it was getting a little late in life to start over. My marriage wasn't doing any better than my career, and I had worked at that, too. I was disappointed in myself. When I was young I had ideals. I wanted to make the world—or at least a small part of it—a better place for all of us to live, but as I got older I began to see that ideals have a hard time surviving. I hadn't taken any meaningful stands if it meant I had to stand alone. I went along with popular decisions even when I didn't believe they were right. I was friendly, but something was missing from my friendships. I did things to please, and I didn't do some things because I was afraid of displeasing. Sometimes I felt that if I suddenly disappeared from the face of the earth, it wouldn't have mattered.

It was during that uneasy time when I was visiting a friend in Washington, D.C. She was deeply involved in a project to improve ghetto housing, and she invited me to sit in on her group's meeting. As we drove across town we were slowed by a lunchtime traffic jam. "We won't have time to look for a garage," my friend said, and before I knew it she began to pray—for a parking space! She was quite businesslike about it. "Lord, You know how important it is for us to get to this meeting on time," she explained. "So will You please help us find a parking space!"

Frankly, I was offended. I thought she was being flippant with God. But I was thoroughly surprised and confused when, a few feet ahead of us, a car pulled away from the curb and we pulled right in. "Thank You, Lord!" my friend said as she turned off the engine.

I stared at her. She looked and sounded the same as she always did, yet there was something different about her. Or, rather, I was seeing something I hadn't seen before. I didn't feel offended anymore, but I was curious.

Later, when we were caught in another traffic jam on our way home, I asked her if she always prayed like that.

"Like what?" she said.

"About—things. Anything . . . little things."

"If they're important to me, I do," she said. She looked at me and smiled. "Don't you?"

"No," I said, and for some reason I felt very sad. "I guess I don't think I ought to."

"That's a shame," she said. "You're really keeping God out of your life that way—and I'm sure He wants to be part of it. Isn't that how you feel when you love somebody?"

I couldn't answer her question then because I needed time to think about it. I knew that God didn't pick up a car and move it out of a space so that we could have it. But I think He had something to do with keeping my friend alert to the possibility of a parking space. And maybe with the timing—did the traffic slow us down just enough to bring us to the right place at the right time? I would never know, and it wasn't important that I did. I wasn't trying to prove that God was powerful, because I already knew that He was. I was trying to find out how I could bring more of that power into my life.

I was very uncomfortable when I began talking to God about such things as emptiness, disappointment, and frustration, but I made myself go on. I told Him how I felt about my work, and how afraid I was to try to make a living doing what I loved. I asked Him to help me keep my marriage together—or else to give me the courage to face my future alone. I asked Him to show me how I could be of some value in this world. I didn't go any further because I started to cry.

I was struggling with feelings of guilt because I didn't think I had the right to talk to God about things that were important to me but might not be to Him. Several times I almost stopped. What enabled me to go on was a gradual awareness of God's closeness—very much like the closeness I used to know in those quiet moments on the lake when the sun was rising. Or the bumpy bus rides with people getting on and off. He literally pushed away the guilt that had come between us. At times He still has to do it, because I never can. But, then, that is what He was trying to teach me: what I can't do, He can. And what I can do, I can do much better with Him.

Power isn't the word for what came into my life. *Love* is. But I don't think there is anything as powerful as love, anyway. God simply wants to help me become the person He originally created me to be. That's what love does. He wants to do more than rescue me. He wants to be in on everything I do, from the beginning to the end. If I've got a reason to be happy, then so does He. If I get hurt, He bleeds. If I want to do something, He'll help me. If I get knocked down, He'll give me some of His strength so I can pick myself up. If I'm worn out, He'll keep me going. If I can't relax, He'll wind me down. Do I need an idea? He'll inspire me. A solution? I can ask Him. He is the Someone who is always there: Christ making good on His promise to go through life with me.

God's love is so different from mine. He can deal with my failures—and those of anybody else—so much better than I can. He doesn't give up on me when I try and try again and still don't succeed. He helps me to look for my mistakes, but He doesn't hold them against me. When I run out of patience with myself—or with anyone else—He offers me His, and we both go at it again. Or we try something else, because with Him I don't feel embarrassed to admit I was wrong. He doesn't think I'm a fool—or a genius, either. I'm a person, and He knows what it is to be one. He also knows what it is to create one. He knows me better than I know myself—but He would like to change that. He would like me to know more about myself so that I can enjoy more of this life He has given me.

You see, I'm not meant to go through life alone—and neither are you. This life, I am beginning to discover, is not a matter of solving some problems and ducking others. It's a learning experience, a course in who we are and where we fit into the world. And Christ is our Teacher.

Years ago, a man I admired very much used to irritate me with his attitude toward problems. "There are no such things as problems," he always said, "only challenges." At the time I was too young and inexperienced to understand what he meant, but I think I understand now. He meant that a problem—any problem—gives us an opportunity to find a solution. And in finding it, we may come upon some ability we didn't know we had—a talent, perhaps, a good idea, a different point of view, a deeper insight, persistence, tough-mindedness, a sense of humor, or the wisdom to ask for help from the right person. Problems aren't meant to trip us up. Very often they can lead to new paths we can take to where we want to go.

And where we want to go is important. Frustrating as it may be when we feel dissatisfied with our lives, those feelings deserve our attention. Because they are whispered pleas from the person God created and wants to help us become. That was one of the first things I learned when I began to share more of my life with God. I was too quick to give up what I wanted, and to settle for what was available. I was too ready to let myself down.

Originally I thought God would quiet my frustration and teach me to accept my limitations. But instead He presented the possibility that I don't have *any* limitations—because I have Him. I can be, not whatever I like, but whatever I truly am. And He will help me.

I was unhappy in my work, in my marriage, and in myself because I wasn't making the best use of what God had given me: Himself. I was making my own way through the world, and I wasn't satisfied with the results. I was a modern-day disciple trying to become a better, more loving, more effective human being, and finding that I just couldn't do it without Christ at my side. I don't know how to deal with my fears. I *need* approval. I don't want to get hurt. I have terrible doubts: *Suppose I fail? What if I'm wrong? What will people say? What will they do? Maybe I'm not good enough, or smart enough, or strong enough.* I see a lot of things that are wrong in this world and I'd like to change some of them, even a little bit, but I'm afraid to try. Unless someone goes with me. That makes all the difference.

When Christ goes with me, He changes me just as He

changed disciples years ago. He makes me bold enough to believe that, even in a troubled world, I can build a life that has purpose, meaning and decency. I can stand alone if I need to, and I can go where there aren't any paths. With Him as my teacher, I can learn how to confront opposition, hostility, deceit and intimidation. He gives me the assurance that I can suffer disapproval if I must, and that however badly I am hurt I can be healed. At times He enables me to be downright pushy when I might ordinarily back down. He finds love in me where I didn't know I had any, and He finds needs for it that I didn't know existed. He is teaching me to be a better friend and a more useful person. He reminds me that there is more to me than meets the eye—there is some of Him in me.

When I was growing up I used to ask my parents to tell me everything they knew about my grandparents, my aunts, uncles and cousins. It was fascinating to be told that I had some of the habits my great-grandmother had. She talked to herself just the way I did; she liked the country even though she lived in the city; and she managed to grow, protect and harvest a spectacular peach tree that took up most of her tiny backyard. Both my mother and father loved to dance, and so did I. Long after I began to scribble poems and stories, I found some poems that my mother had written as a young girl and was too shy to show me. I liked knowing I took after someone. It taught me something about myself. Later on I began to realize that in many ways I was different from any of my relatives, as each of us is. I didn't mind that. In fact, during my teens and twenties I probably made too much of a fuss about it. One of my goals in life was to find and to be the "real" me. I immersed myself in books, courses and quizzes that were supposed to tell me who I was and why. And in some ways they did, although it wasn't like being related to someone.

But there is more to me than my biological heredity and my individuality. There is a spiritual part of me, and I need God to explain it to me. Because we are related, He and I. He has been human, and I—since He is a part of me—am at least somewhat divine. Or, rather, I can be if I am willing to let Him teach me how to use the spiritual part of myself in this world.

What, for instance, can I do with the hurt I feel when someone lies to me? How can I pursue a dream when reality keeps telling me it's not worth the effort? What can I do about a mistake I made? How can I help a friend who is troubled? Is there any way I can stop someone from doing something wrong? How can I be more patient with someone who rubs me the wrong way? Where can I find the courage to stand up to somebody who is bigger than I am? How can I make someone I love happy? How do I know I'm right? What will I have to give up to get what I want out of life? What can I do when I'm afraid—of getting sick, of getting old, of dying?

Only God can answer these questions for me because He has had to answer them for Himself. He has had to live in this world and to meet its challenges. And He knows that by meeting them we discover who we are and what we can do. We get a sense of our own worth.

We learn from God what to do about a lie. How to make ourselves heard. When to be still. When to give and when to take. How much. When to strike a blow, and how to take as many as come our way. Where to go for help and when to give some. What to do when the other guy is bigger, tougher and meaner than we are. By learning how to take care of

Preface

ourselves, we will know how to take care of one another. By being loved, we will know how to love. And that is what we are here to do.

I know now that I cannot—and never will—get through a single day or a single moment of the rest of my life without the loving presence of the God who made me. He is as essential to my life here on earth as He is to any life I may have hereafter. It is *His* strength, which He puts in *my* hands, that gives me the confidence to change my life—and my world.

At no single moment in my life did I begin to live boldly. It happened slowly—because it is one thing to realize that we have access to God's power, and something else to use it. I couldn't simply go out into the world and put my spiritual strength to work. I still had the same fears, the same doubts about myself. I had to let *God* change the way I think before *I* could change the way I live. I had to realize that I am not here all by myself. I had to learn, from God Himself, that faith, trust and love are not words of comfort, but the strength and energy we all need to make our way in the world. I had to discover that God knows me better than anyone else does. And I had to know that He wouldn't let me down. Ever. Only then did I have the courage to begin becoming the person God had always meant me to be.

I don't take small helpings of God's love anymore. I take as much as my life can hold. I include Him in on everything—not only my problems, but my hopes, my disappointments, my feelings, my thoughts, my work, all my relationships, my good times and bad times. He and I are in this life together, and my life has been much more meaningful since I realized that. He enables me to live boldly, and I believe that is what He created all of us to do.

Chapter 1

❧

Faith Is More Than Believing

I USED TO THINK that faith was something I had to do—about God. But it isn't that way at all. Faith is something God does—about me. He becomes involved in my life.

I remember how guilty I felt many years ago when I thought I had run out of faith. I was in my junior year of college and I woke up one morning with a high fever, which was unusual for me. I tried to ignore it and attended my classes, but when I came home at the end of the day I was so weak that my mother sent for a doctor. Since I was hardly ever ill, I was stunned by the diagnosis: rheumatic fever.

The doctor was very kind, very sympathetic, as he described to my parents and me how my illness would affect my life. I would have to spend about a year in bed, flat on my back. Most of my food would be taken in the form of fluids. There might be damage to my heart. Of course, I would have to drop out of school. The doctor also suggested that it might not be wise for me to plan on marriage and motherhood.

I sat up all night. I had promised my mother that the

next morning I would lie flat on my back and drink through a bent straw. But since I *was* able to sit up, I wanted to do it for a few more hours so I could remember how it felt.

This is where my faith should help me, I thought, and in those days I defined faith quite simply: I believed in God. Faith meant that there was more to life than I could see and touch and do. There was—somewhere—a spiritual place to which I could retreat when things got a little rough here on earth. God would be there waiting to comfort me when no one else could. As I sat up through that long night, I tried desperately hard to find that place, and I couldn't. There was no comfort for me. Only anger and panic.

I wanted so much to be brave, and I knew I wasn't. I imagined how I would behave if I really had faith: reassuring my parents, smiling to my friends, making jokes with the doctor and the nurses who would be coming in to help my mother look after me. Surely I would find something worthwhile in a terrible experience.

I apologized to God because I thought my emotions were getting in the way of my faith. Yet the more I tried to control them, the more insistent they became. My anger, particularly. I felt miserable—but not so miserable that I couldn't sit up. I wasn't the least bit hungry, but if I had to eat, I wanted to do it with a knife, a fork and a spoon, not a straw. I wanted to fight back instead of surrender, and to me that seemed wrong. I expected faith to make me submissive, and since I was anything but submissive, I thought I didn't have faith. I prayed for it passionately, but all I got in return was a stronger determination to fight. And the odd thing is, I am not, and never have been, much of a fighter.

So where, then, was this determination coming from? Obviously God was not trying to calm me down. If anything,

He was as angry as I was. No wonder I hadn't been able to find that distant domain of comfort—comfort wasn't what I needed. I also didn't need to go looking for God. He came looking for me.

It was His nearness, His understanding of what I felt, that taught me to respect the emotions that are a vital part of me. They aren't meant to get in my way. They are the sparks that grow out of my contact with reality. They tell me what is going on, and urge me to react.

The next morning I reacted. I sought another medical opinion. The result was a battery of tests that proved I did *not* have rheumatic fever. My symptoms were similar, but they came from an abscess under a tooth that was quite healthy and did not ache. After a visit to my dentist, and some antibiotics to relieve an infection, I began to regain my strength by the hour. Three days later I was fine—not because I was able to find God and be comforted by Him, but because God found me and shared my anger. He, too, was urging me to react.

Then I realized that God had already given me every-thing I needed to deal with the crisis I faced. I had His presence and understanding—no question about that. But now it was up to me to *do* something with the power He put in my hands. I didn't have to accept my situation.

Now I know that faith is more than knowing God exists. It is letting Him into my life.

Be Prepared to Change

On my own, there really is very little that I can do about my life. I am only one person, and my life touches so many others. It also collides with lives that are going in different directions. Events happen. Situations develop. And I can't always control them. Sometimes they turn my life completely around, forcing me to take detours. I can't expect to be prepared for all I may meet along the way. Some of my best plans may have to be put aside. Some of my dearest dreams will not come true.

I can, if I choose, play it safe. I can stop planning and stop dreaming. I can try to avoid anything that is bigger and stronger than I am. I can go around it, or go along with it. I can hunker down along the edges of life where anything threatening might not notice me.

Or—I can live by faith. I can walk through this world with God.

It will not be a placid journey. I will not get through life without a scratch. I will meet many of the same events and situations I would meet if I were traveling alone—but I will deal with them in different ways. I may want to avoid them, but I won't, because God doesn't have to play it safe and He will lead me into encounters I would never attempt by myself. I'll win some and lose some, but either way I'll learn something about myself. I'll discover my strengths and my weaknesses. I'll have a better sense of what I can and cannot do. I'll stop being so afraid of getting hurt because I'll know I can be healed. I'll stop worrying about failing, because I'll realize it's only a step backward, and I can always go forward again. Whatever I achieve, whatever successes I may have, it will never be empty; there will always be something to do with it, someone with whom I can share it. God will show me what to do with all the love and all the care I am about to discover in myself. I will become a useful person in a needy world.

How? By letting God explain me to myself. By letting Him teach me how to make better use of what He has given me. By letting Him show me options I didn't know I had. He has been here. He has gone through everything you and I will ever do. We can learn from His experience.

We look at things so differently, God and I. I see only what I have to do; He sees choices. I let life push me around; He knows I can push back. Once I start something, I try to finish it; He reminds me that sometimes it's a good idea to try something new. I worry about all the mistakes I've made; He thinks maybe I've learned something from them. I don't like to play hardball; He's good at it. I want to be a success; He thinks I ought to enjoy what I do. I want to be self-sufficient; He knows I need help.

This much I know already: the presence of God is going to change the way I live.

Becoming a Choosy Person

Do you try to make the best of things? I always did. But not anymore. With God's help, I am becoming a choosy person. I don't always settle for what I am given—at least not since I learned that sometimes I can do better.

One summer morning some years ago, I left my house as three painters were setting up their ladders to do the second story trim. I was gone all day. At sunset, as I turned into my driveway, I couldn't believe what I saw. One of the ladders, a huge, telescoping thing, was braced against the front of my house, leading up to my guest room window. No one was in sight. The painters' truck was gone. Obviously they had forgotten the ladder.

At the time, I was living in a small house on a very busy road. I didn't like the ladder and its access to a window being visible to so many passing strangers.

I let myself into the house and went straight to the phone. There was no answer at the painters' number. I took a closer look at the ladder, and it was bigger than I thought. When I gripped both sides and tugged, it wouldn't budge. All three sections were fully extended, and I was afraid that if somehow I managed to pull the upper sections down where they belonged, the whole thing might fall over and crush me.

I went back to the phone and called everyone I knew—and no one was home. My neighbors were away. Apparently I would just have to get through the night with that ladder leading up to a window.

Oh, no, I wouldn't!

It was getting dark and I had to work quickly. I couldn't lift the ladder, but perhaps I could pull it away from the house and let it fall in the opposite direction. Except that there was a telephone wire stretching across the opposite direction. The ladder would have to fall at a very peculiar angle, or cause a lot of damage.

I must have gained some strength from my desperation because I was able to pull the ladder out from the wall, just far enough for me to slip between it and the house. It was already starting to fall in the opposite direction, and as it went I pushed as hard as I could toward my left. The ladder barely missed the wire and came down with a terrible rattling crash. It didn't seem to be broken, and I dragged it inch by inch into a line of bushes where it was almost hidden. I stood there, breathing heavily and covered with a paintlike dust, but knowing I would enjoy a good night's sleep.

The next morning, when the painters showed up, they couldn't believe what I told them. But I knew what had happened, and it changed the way I regarded myself. Until then I hadn't considered myself to be physically strong. I've been blessed with good health all my life, but I'm not a big person. I had also grown up in a culture that assumed women were fragile. So, to my mind, there were certain things I couldn't expect to do. Or even try. Now I knew better.

Not that I'm looking for more ladders to topple. Or trying to prove that I can handle anything that comes along. But I am open to the possibility that I can do something about myself, my life and my world. I don't always have to put up with the debris that others leave in my life. Or even with my own debris. God has made me aware that I have a choice.

Pushing Back at Life

Sometimes, just when we need patience and understanding, life shoves us aside as if we didn't matter. But that doesn't mean we have to get out of life's way. We *can* push back. I learned something about that from a little boy.

He was six, maybe seven, years old when I met him. He was big for his age and clumsy, all feet and hands thrashing out. He was hyperkinetic, meaning that he was driven by a fierce amount of energy that made it impossible for him to sit still. He was also dyslexic, meaning that he didn't see the world the way most of us do. Sometimes words and numbers appeared to him upside down or backwards, sometimes in a hopeless tangle no one could decipher. He was a problem in school, always getting out of his seat and moving around, struggling to read the simplest word or sentence, and stuttering when he tried to speak, his words tumbling out in stops and starts. Some people—a lot, actually—thought he was stupid. He wasn't. Not at all. His brain played tricks on him—which is what dyslexia does—but it was an excellent brain. Underneath all that confusion of noise and motion was a remarkable intelligence. And that was the cruelest part of it all, because the boy was aware that something was wrong. He knew, or at least he thought he did, that he wasn't what so many people said he was: a pest, incorrigible, dumb, destructive, an impossible child. He was loving, expressive, and very much in need of love, except that what he did and what he said didn't come out that way.

The next time I saw him he was twenty-three, and we were working together professionally. He was writing a book about the experience of being dyslexic, and I was his editor. He could sit still by then, although he often tapped the heel of one foot on the floor in a rapid rhythm. He didn't stutter and, in fact, he spoke almost as eloquently as he wrote. He worked at a battered old portable typewriter that he treated with great respect, and as he finished each chapter he sent it on to me. Sometimes he drove the two hundred miles between his home and my office to hand me a few chapters at a time, and he would wait quietly, but intently, while I read them. He would revise, then and there, using the old portable, which he always brought with him. He preferred it to my spiffier electric model.

His work needed polish, but it was evident from the first few pages that he was a natural writer with an enormous talent. And so eager to learn! He took my suggestions hungrily and always came back with something far better than I had in mind.

The book James S. Evans wrote, *An Uncommon Gift,* answered the question I wanted to ask him. How did he manage to get control of his life?

"Self-discipline," he said. As if it were something for everyone.

But that's just it. It is.

Most of us think of self-discipline as a way to correct what is wrong with us. And it isn't. Self-discipline is the struggle to be ourselves—no matter what others expect of us. It is Mary knowing she is the mother of God's Son, and therefore refusing to live in shame. It is Peter daring to come out of hiding because he knows he is not a coward. It is so many nobodies turning the world around. It is a little boy growing into a loving human being instead of a bitter, hostile reject. We all need self-discipline.

It wasn't easy for Jamie to push back when life disabled him. His parents understood what his problem was, and they loved him. It was a little harder for his brothers and his sister because Jamie, in his rage at being "different," became adept at making them miserable. But very few others tried to understand Jamie; they did their best to avoid him. All they wanted him to do was stay out of their way. Finally, at his young age, Jamie had to make a decision that comes to most of us much later: What kind of a person was he going to be? The sensitive, intelligent, compassionate person God created?—or the rebellious outcast? Was he going to demand that other people understand him? Or was he going to try to understand himself?

Jamie's parents leveled with him. He could work with

tutors after school, he could put in many more hours on his homework than other kids did, he could learn to translate the gibberish he saw into the words, letters and numbers other children saw, he could manage to sit still until a class ended, he could work off some of his energy through strenuous exercise, and he could hope to make progress slowly, painfully, but eventually. By going over and over the same letters, words and sentences until he cried with frustration, he would learn how they were supposed to look, in spite of the way they appeared to him. And once he did that, he could communicate who he was. He could put his ideas into words that other people could understand. He could begin to have friendships. He could think about his future, about what he wanted to do and where he wanted to go—just like anyone else. Or—he could stay mad at the world for the rest of his life.

Jamie chose to become himself, no matter how much work it took. That's what self-discipline is.

Being a Flexible Person

How often someone will say to me, "It must be wonderful to work at home!" It's not my favorite comment.

I can guess what they're thinking: I can sleep as long as I please, I don't have to get dressed up, I don't have to commute, I work only when I'm in the mood, and my time is my own.

I'm often tempted to defend myself. To explain that I keep to a schedule, that I'm at my desk at a certain hour every morning, that I work all day and sometimes all evening, that I don't stop to raid the refrigerator or make personal calls or visit my friends, and if anyone comes to my door unexpectedly, he or she is not welcome. When I work, I'm out of touch with the rest of my world.

But usually I decide to say nothing in my defense because I realize that I really *am* fortunate to work at home. It's where I like to be, and if I'm needed, at least I'm there. It spares me the tug-of-war so many women—especially young women—experience when they are torn between their career and their family. The way my mother was.

My mother never got over the guilt she felt for leaving me in the care of someone else while she went to work. It was harder for her than it would be now, because in those days very few women worked outside their home. My mother felt conspicuous, but she didn't know what to do about it. She began working before I was born. She and my father were very young and neither of them earned enough money to support a home and a family. But when my mother no longer had to work, she kept on. She needed to do more than look after me and our home.

Once, after I began to go to school, she took a two-year leave of absence and stayed home. She cleaned the house mercilessly, she was always there for me, and she even made grape jam—more than we could eat in a year. But she was unhappy. She rarely smiled, and when she hugged me her eyes told me that she was far, far away. Eventually she resumed her career, and as she ran out the door that first morning back on the job, I could sense her happiness. I felt closer to her than at any time when she was home with me. Unfortunately, I was never able to find the words to convince her that by meeting her own needs, she wasn't ignoring mine. She carried her guilt with her until the day she died.

I suffer some of the same guilt whenever my work takes

me away from home for days at a time. I feel as if I'm doing something wrong by leaving my loved ones behind, even though I arrange for them to get the best of care. I feel as if I'm depriving them of me.

And yet, I'm not. I'm leaving with them the mothering part of me, and that will never go away. It's there in the care they are getting, even though someone else is giving it to them. It's there in my concern for their well-being, for the fact that I am always only a telephone call away. I take with me only what I need for the work I have to do: my professional abilities.

It amazes me to find that Christ Himself can help me to understand this conflict of responsibilities between my work and my family. Yet He certainly was torn by them at least as much as you and I are. Perhaps He liked being a carpenter in a small town where everyone knew everyone. We know He cared deeply about His family. It must have been difficult for Him to leave and go into a busy metropolitan area, but that's where His work took Him. Sitting among theologians in the temple, under attack for what He preached, He was a patient, considerate teacher. To the vendors and money-changers, He was a dangerous crusader. To the men and women who sheltered Him and followed Him from town to town, He was a trusted friend. To the Romans He was a fool. To the sick and the dying He was a healer. To the lost, He was a savior.

He was so many different things to so many different people—but not all at the same time. Yet to each one He gave something of Himself that was needed, and it stayed with them.

I am beginning to realize that I don't have to give up one part of myself in order to satisfy the other. I can use the talents God has given me as long as I use them where and when they are needed. I can be Martha to my family and Mary to my career. I can be gentle with a friend, yet fierce in my protest against injustice. I can be a patient teacher, but intolerant of bigotry. I can be concerned over the future, and still laugh about something that happened yesterday.

God has given me flexibility.

If I could, I would tell my mother that when she went out the door those many mornings, she didn't leave me. The part of her that I needed was with me all the time. And I'm sure that the people who worked with her felt the same way when she left the office and went home. She just didn't realize that it was all right to be flexible—and I wish she had.

Something Right out of Something Wrong

The worst part about the mistakes we make is that we go on living with them. Even if no one else knows about them, we don't feel the same way about ourselves. We're uncomfortable with our faults. They make us less lovable—and we need all the love we can get.

Wayne made some mistakes, but with the best of intentions. He loved his family and wanted to give them everything—fast. He had talent, no doubt about it. He could write the kind of ad copy that made people want to buy anything. He knew that sometimes he was persuading people to buy something that wasn't worth what they paid for it. Sometimes he explained a contract or a guarantee or a policy in terms that promised things that didn't exist. It bothered him, but when he got that worried look on his face his boss took him out for a big lunch, a couple of drinks and the promise of a raise. Someday, his boss told him, Wayne was going to become a partner in the business.

That pleased Wayne. He wanted to get ahead quickly, not only for the money but because he wanted to have more time for the kind of writing that was important to him. He was a history buff. He spent every spare hour researching a little-known Revolutionary War battle and he was writing a book about it. The manuscript was a rough draft, but it was good enough to make him think he could finish it someday. Why not now? his wife asked. Why not look for a less demanding job and work on the book at night? No, Wayne told her, there wasn't enough money in it.

The next time Wayne's boss took him out to lunch he said he was going to start his own agency and asked Wayne to come with him. Wayne was excited. The offer looked like a shortcut to everything he wanted.

Starting up a new agency meant longer hours and less money, but Wayne believed what his boss told him: things would get better. Soon. Wayne was drinking more, but he blamed it on the pressure. He was sure he could stop anytime he wanted. His wife was worried, and they argued a lot. Every now and then Wayne would take out his unfinished manuscript and read it. It was just as good as he remembered. Maybe better. He'd get back to it. But first he had to put bread on the table.

You can imagine how Wayne felt when his boss called him into his office one day and told him that his copy just wasn't what it used to be. It wasn't persuasive. It wasn't original. It didn't have that spark. And if Wayne couldn't give the clients what they wanted, there were plenty of people out there who could.

Wayne was scared. He took a look at the copy his boss

had turned back to him and he couldn't see anything wrong with it. It was the same kind of copy his boss used to think was terrific. Maybe there were the same phrases here and there, maybe the same gimmicks to catch the reader's attention. But they were good phrases, good gimmicks. Wayne kept using them because he knew they worked.

What he needed, Wayne told himself, was someone who appreciated him, the way his boss once did. In fact, he blamed his boss for several things: for underpaying him, for talking him into leaving a job with a better agency, and now for trying to undermine his self-confidence. He added to the list every night when he stopped for a few drinks on the way home.

On the day Wayne got fired, he went home early. No one was there. He went upstairs and took his manuscript out of the desk drawer. Then he brought it down to the family room. He lit some logs in the fireplace, and when they glowed beneath the flames, he picked up his manuscript and threw it in.

When Wayne's wife came home from work she found him sitting on the floor in front of the fireplace, rocking back and forth in pain. His hands were badly burned, but he was holding his manuscript against his chest and sobbing. Only the edges of the manuscript were charred because almost as soon as he threw it into the fire he reached in to pull it out.

"I couldn't destroy it," he told his wife. "It's the best part of me."

How do you live with your mistakes? You don't. You take the best part of yourself—the part God sees so much more clearly than you do—and you go on from there. The way Mary Magdalene did. Or Zacchaeus. Or any of the rest of us. In time, that part of you, however small it was to begin with, grows—until it becomes your whole way of life.

Wayne can tell you about that. He still writes persuasive copy, although he doesn't make as much money doing it. He free-lances, which gives him a chance to say no to assignments he can't believe in. He's building a new reputation that way—some people say that if Wayne writes something, then it must be true. The manuscript? It's almost finished. Wayne's pretty proud of it.

He hasn't forgotten the mistakes he made, or the pain they caused him. But he stopped living with them. Now he lives with something he didn't have before: his own respect—for the person he really is. For the person God saw all along.

Setting Realistic Goals

When I was in college, I applied for a Fulbright scholarship. It wasn't my idea because, frankly, I wasn't *that* good a student. But my faculty advisor thought I might have a chance, as long as I chose to study at a foreign university that wasn't very well known. "Don't aim for the University of Edinburgh," he said, "because every other English major wants to go there, and very few will. Pick a place like the Gobi desert, and you won't run into so much competition."

But the University of Edinburgh was the only place where I wanted to go, and that's what I selected. I was not awarded a scholarship, and my advisor was disappointed in me. "You've got to match your goals to your talent," he told me. "That's how to win in this world."

He had a point, and I think I benefited from his advice. But he left something out: in order to set realistic goals, we have to know more about ourselves than how much talent we have. We also have to know what our spiritual needs are. Because unless those needs are satisfied, we will never find joy in achieving our goals. Perhaps this is what Christ was trying to explain to us in the Beatitudes—that what we give to life is as important to our well-being as what we get from it.

A friend of mine—her name is Terry—would agree. And she is the most goal-oriented person I've ever known.

Terry has a lot of talents. She's an artist, a teacher, a mother, a businesswoman, a homemaker. She's also a tender, compassionate, generous woman. She planned to develop all those abilities, a few at a time. First she was going to find the right man and get married. Then she would have a family. She would continue to paint whenever she had the time, but when the children went to school, she would give more of her attention to art. She might even teach. It was a fine plan. Very realistic.

Almost according to schedule, Terry met Dennis, a charming, intelligent, fun-loving man. They got married and had two children. Dennis was a reporter for a large metro-politan newspaper, and his work took him all over the world. Sometimes Terry and the children went with him. It was a fascinating life until Dennis came down with "some-thing" that left him weak and listless. His attacks came and went. Finally he was diagnosed as having Parkinson's disease. There could be no cure, but with the proper medication Dennis would hope to live for several years.

"The shock was bad enough," Terry says, "but I could have lived with that. What was worse was the way Dennis changed. He was scared." He would sit at his desk for hours, drinking and staring at a blank piece of paper. Then he would go into a rage. "I could get out of his way," Terry said, "but the kids couldn't. He hurt them, badly. Eventually, the only peace we had was when one of his attacks put him in the hospital. I knew we couldn't go on that way."

Seeing the fear in the eyes of her son and daughter, Terry finally came to a painful decision: she and the children had to leave Dennis. "It took me a long time to do it," she remembers. "I suppose I kept hoping that one day Dennis would be the man he used to be. My faith means a lot to me, and in my faith you just don't walk out on a marriage. Sometimes, when Dennis was in bad shape, I'd wonder who would look after him if I wasn't there. Still—I had to think of the kids."

Terry's mother and father supported her decision. So did Dennis's sister. Together they arranged for Dennis to enter a nursing home where Terry knew he would get the medical care he needed. "It was expensive," Terry explains. "I couldn't have done it by myself."

Terry immediately set new goals for herself. She had sold a painting occasionally, but that wasn't enough to support her and the children, and to pay for her share of Dennis's care. She decided to open a small framing shop where she could also offer art classes. The combination worked. She didn't make a lot of money, but she got along.

Dennis accused Terry of abandoning him. "He screamed at me every time I visited him," she says. "So—I didn't go very often. I think I finally realized that the change in his personality was permanent. Maybe my kids realized it sooner than I did because they refused to see him at all. But I felt so guilty about them—I knew it hurt them to hate their father."

As the years passed, the children grew up, finished school and were happy in their work. Terry was about to take life a little easier. Then, about a year ago, Terry had a call from Dennis's doctor. Since they were never divorced, Terry was still Dennis's next of kin. It was time, the doctor said, to seek some kind of terminal care for Dennis. Could Terry suggest anything?

To everyone's surprise, Terry brought Dennis into her own home. She built a small addition onto the first floor so that Dennis could have a place of his own. A ramp leads to the backyard and he can wheel himself outside in good weather.

During the day practical nurses look after Dennis while Terry runs her shop. She puts in long hours, but doesn't seem to mind. She still sees her friends. She still paints. Sometimes she spends the evening with Dennis, reading to him or watching television. "He's too sick to hurt anyone now," Terry says.

Sometimes the children come to visit. "At first I think they only came to see if I was all right. They wouldn't even talk to Dennis. But after a while they began to realize how frightened he is—he's the way they were when they were little and he was out of control. They know it doesn't make any sense to hate him anymore—and for that, I'm grateful! Last month my kids surprised me with a birthday party, and they included Dennis."

But why did Terry bring Dennis back into her life? What about her own goals?

"I wouldn't enjoy taking life easy right now," she says. "I care what happens to Dennis—and I care *how* it happens."

Terry didn't abandon her goals. But she adjusted them to suit the kind of person she is. Because sometimes we need to do more than achieve what we want out of life. Sometimes we just need to give. And we have to take that into account when we set our goals.

Playing Hardball

When it comes to sports, I enjoy seeing two good teams go at each other with everything they've got. Even if the teams aren't well matched, I like to see both teams play as well as they can.

When it comes to life, I seem to play by different rules. If I'm in conflict with someone who is as strong as I am, I tend to go a little easy on him. If I'm up against someone much stronger, I often give up without a fight. I don't like to play hardball.

Why?

I could say that I don't believe in taking life so seriously. That there's no point in making a big fuss over a difference of opinion or a conflict of ideas. That I'd rather be liked than be victorious. Except that I don't think any of these reasons are true.

I don't like to play hardball because I'm afraid of getting hurt. Maybe even getting killed.

But, you say, those things don't really happen, do they?

Yes. They do.

I can show you the scars: from the time I won the struggle and lost the friend I defeated. And the time my opponent played as hard as I did and turned out to be stronger and more durable than I was; my career suffered from that one. Or the time I played beautifully, even though my opponent was weaker than I was—and some people thought I was unfair.

But how can anyone get killed playing hardball? By being perceived as a different kind of person. Playing hard—whether you win or lose—means the death of your reputation as Ms. or Mr. Nice. Now you're someone to be reckoned with. And that's not always comfortable.

I've tried to avoid situations that lead to playing hardball, and sometimes I've succeeded. But I don't like the way I feel. I don't like agreeing to something that I don't believe. It hurts me, more than getting hurt myself, when I see someone getting bullied and I don't do anything to help. I can't respect myself when I allow anyone to take advantage of me.

Why, then, don't I ask Christ to keep me out of trouble? The fact is that I do. And He doesn't. Since Christ is in my life, I not only play hardball more often—but I'm getting better at it.

Looking at life through His eyes, I have to take it much more seriously. I can't allow someone to make a derogatory remark about a person or a group and assume that I agree with him simply because I'm silent. I have to speak up. I can't watch some people poison this earth and say nothing because I don't want them to think I'm a kook. I have to alert them, and, if necessary, try to stop them. I can't overlook dishonesty even though it seems to be everywhere. I have to oppose it—beginning with my own way of life.

I can't allow a friend to put off paying me for work I have done. I can't ignore promises that are made and broken. I can't suppress an opinion because someone I value may not agree with it. I can't change what I am in order to live up to someone's expectations. I can't allow anyone, however well intentioned, to persuade me to give up what I believe. I must be willing to fight for the right to think for myself.

Yes, there are many reasons to play hardball.

And the dangers? They haven't diminished. I get hurt, very often. But I have learned something else from having Christ in my life. *I recover.* There is, in every wound, a possibility for resurrection. Sometimes it's the relief of discovering that I can speak my mind, not in anger but in love. Sometimes, even though my opponent turns a deaf ear to my pleas, someone else hears and I meet a new friend. Sometimes I feel better just knowing that I can survive being hurt. And sometimes I even win.

Getting the Help We Need

Whenever I am deeply troubled, it helps me to talk to someone who understands how I feel. Whenever I'm wrestling with a problem that seems to be bigger than I am, I begin to think there is something wrong with me. Then, when I talk to other people about it, I find that I'm not alone after all. Everybody has problems, some bigger than mine. That doesn't solve my problem, but at least it tells me that I'm a normal human being who's going through a difficult time. For some reason, I feel stronger knowing that I'm like other people.

When good things happen, I can't wait to share the news. But not with just anybody. It has to be someone who understands how much this happiness means to me. Someone who has suffered with me, waited with me, tried and failed with me—and now can be as happy as I am.

Unfortunately, I cannot have these wonderful people with me all the time. Or at the exact moment when I need them the most. They have their own lives and their own concerns, and they aren't always available.

I do, however, have Someone who is with me at all times. Someone who knows me better than anyone else in the world. Someone who has so lovingly shared all of my life that He can appreciate exactly what each moment means to me. I have God.

When I was a child I tried very hard not to be afraid of thunderstorms. My mother was terrified of them, but she did her best to hide her fear, and I wanted her to think she succeeded. So the two of us would sit by a window in a darkened room, looking out into the lightning-slashed sky as if it were a show that nature was putting on for us alone. My mother would hold me close to her, and sometimes I could feel a trembling in her arms. I thought it was funny that a grownup should be afraid.

Now that I'm a grownup, I find that I'm afraid of many things in this world. Now, when there's a thunderstorm, I don't go near a window. I know that lightning is dangerous. And if lightning doesn't get me, something else might—an accident, disease, violence, war, an ugly word, laughter at the wrong time, separation, deceit. The list is endless, and what bothers me is that there doesn't seem to be anything I can do about these threats to my well-being. Being an adult hasn't given me the power I thought I would have. It has simply made me aware of how dangerous a place this world is. And how very small I am. I could never get through it without God.

He doesn't shield me from life. I have tasted sorrow, disappointment, frustration and defeat. I have knuckled under to disease and misunderstandings, and death has stolen loved ones from me. I have seen right wrestled to the ground and wrong raised up to be adored. I get out alive because I call on God for help. Somehow He makes it possible for me to do what I can't do on my own. Whatever I need, He always gives me. When I'm afraid, His hand is always there for me to hold onto for dear life. When I'm hurt, He teaches me how to clench my teeth until the pain goes away—and then He heals me. When I think no one cares, He envelops me in His arms until I have to believe I am important to Him. He leads me into many a worthy battle, even though sometimes we both know we are going to lose. At exactly the right moment He brings special people into my life.

If I have to make a decision, He can cut through the red tape of my excuses and show me where my choices lie. If I hunger for friendship, He doesn't bring me a friend—He teaches me how to *be* one. If my courage is running low, He lends me some of His. If I'm depressed by all the mistakes I've made, He reminds me of a few things I've done right. I can even talk to God about money or, rather, the lack of it, and know that He understands my anxiety. No, He doesn't present me with a windfall, but He renews my patience by calling my attention to some more enduring treasures in my life.

Faith—this presence of God in our lives—is not a promise that the storms will go away. It is God teaching us how to get through them: how to deal with the unexpected, with the plans that don't work, with the dreams that don't come true, with the bad breaks, with our own poor judgment—and even with the kick in the shins.

But faith is more than an attitude. It is a call to action, a reminder that we have options, not limitations. Faith is God's way of assuring us that we have the power to change our lives for the better, no matter what our situation.

I know a woman who is in danger of dying because she refuses to take charge of her life. She has been hurt. As a child, she was denied love and care, ridiculed when she desperately needed encouragement, ignored when she was hungry for understanding. She has not had a good life. But she continues to insist that, somewhere, some one person is going to rescue her from her pain. She refuses to accept the possibility that God has already given her what she needs to rescue herself. In the middle years of her life, she is still the injured, weeping child who wants a wizard with a magic wand to make her unhappiness go away in a shimmer of golden light. And so she waits, convinced that God has forgotten her.

This is a lovely woman I am describing. She is capable of caring deeply. She has a good mind and a lot of grit in her. She has, in fact, everything she is seeking from someone else, but she will not use it.

There has been no rescue, and no rescuer. Only false hopes and cruel disappointments. In her rage over her unhappiness, she has tried to end her life. Twice that I know of. One of these times she may succeed. And we all will have cause to mourn the woman who might have been. She would have added to our lives if only she had taken charge of her own.

I can't help but wonder what my life might have been if I had taken charge of it long ago. If I had acted on my faith a little earlier. If I had taken more risks, been more responsible. If I hadn't taken some advice. If I had taken some more seriously. I'm sure I would have made mistakes—but different ones. And perhaps not the same ones over and over. I might have had more courage, more confidence. I might have been more successful, and that would be nice.

I also might have been badly hurt, more than once. Who knows how many people I trusted would have let me down. As much as I might have achieved, I might have lost it all trying to save someone. And maybe the person I was trying to save would turn around and tell me to mind my own business. The people I love probably would agree. I might have lost a few friends. And made some enemies.

So, why would I want to do such a thing? Why would I want to take charge of my life? What's in it for me?

The freedom to be all that I am. The discovery that I have abilities I haven't yet used. Talents to meet needs that have gone hungry. Ways to communicate with people I would like very much to know. Solutions for problems I have carried around too long. Endurance to get me through the hard times. Compassion when nothing else can help. Healing for my wounds. The satisfaction of knowing that I don't have to wait for anyone to do for me what I can very well do for myself. Joy when there is no earthly reason for it.

Oh, yes, there's a lot in it for me.

Chapter 2

Trust Him to Understand

"TRUST ME."

We've all heard that before—and said it, too. We meant well, and so did those in whom we placed our trust. The words were a solemn promise: "I'll take care of you."

And then something went wrong. We got hurt. Or we did the hurting.

Someone was late for an important appointment. Someone didn't show up at all. Someone gave you the wrong directions and you got lost. Someone who usually understood you didn't even have time to listen. Someone who said he'd stand up for you, didn't.

Or maybe you told a friend you'd always be there if she needed you—except that you didn't expect her to need money. Maybe someone took your advice about demanding a raise—and lost a job. Maybe you assured a child that if you let go, he would float on the water—and then you had to pull him out, gagging and coughing, with that awful accusation in his eyes.

After a while, we come to the conclusion that trust isn't something we can count on. We may want to take care of

27

each other, but we can't. We may want to hold someone up, but we're not as strong as we thought. We may wish we could solve someone's problems, but we're not wise enough.

God doesn't have our shortcomings, so there really isn't any reason why we can't trust Him to lead us safely through this world. And yet we don't. At least, not all of the time.

Does that mean that we don't think we can count on God?

When I began to live by faith, I thought trust would come naturally to me. I expected that, when God beckoned, I would respond the way Samuel did when he awoke to a voice calling his name in the middle of the night. Or Peter summoned by a stranger on the shore to leave his nets behind and go fishing in other waters. I thought I would simply go wherever God led, without question. But that isn't what happened.

For one thing, God didn't beckon. He led me in much more subtle ways: a nudge here, an uneasiness there, a door opening—or closing—a word someone said that lingers in the mind, an insight into something that once made no sense, an unexplainable calm in the midst of anxiety. Sometimes He communicated while I was praying—He was that close. Nevertheless, I wasn't always certain that I understood what He meant. Especially when He urged me to do something risky. Or to go where I was afraid to go. Sometimes I didn't do anything. It seemed safer that way. Or sometimes I went my own way instead of His, because it seemed like a better idea. And, once again, God had to come and rescue me.

I had so many questions I wanted to ask Him, but I kept them to myself. I thought that if I had questions, it meant I didn't trust God—because trust meant following Him blindly. Without hesitation. Without swallowing hard. Without hearing your heart pound in your head.

If ever there was a time when I needed to count on God, it was when I was putting my life together after my marriage ended. I was living in a new community, making new friends, and giving much more serious attention to my career. Everything about my life was different from the way it had been. I had so many decisions to make, and very little confidence in my judgment. And I had *so* many questions—not about God, but about me. Not, Where was He leading me?—but, Would I be able to follow? Would I be able to survive there? Who would look after me if I needed help? Would I be happy—ever—again?

My most important decision concerned my career, because I had to provide for my future as a single woman. Should I take a full-time job (with its comfortable fringe benefits), start a small business (with the help of some interested investors), or continue the chancy life of a writer? Doors opened to all three.

I knew what I wanted. I had worked long and hard to become a writer. I had given it up many times and gone back into a full-time job, only to find that I had to try once more. But it was different being on my own. I felt I needed a steady income rather than the seesaw kind of money a writer makes.

It seemed to me that God ought to understand my doubts and fears even though I didn't mention them. I expected Him to lead me into something secure because, obviously, that was what I needed. Well, of course, He did—but He also threw in an opportunity to edit a book. It was a book that interested me, but it would have taken all my working time. And when it was finished, what then?

Writers always have to deal with "What then?" which is why I was trying not to be one.

The pressure to make a decision was more than I could handle—when something else happened. For thirteen years I had loved a feisty, delightful Welsh Terrier named Trooper. And when so much in my life demanded that I be toughminded and self-sufficient, Trooper was always there to remind me that there was a softer, more vulnerable part of me. It was, in fact, his steady devotion that helped me get through many upheavals. He had always been a healthy dog—then suddenly he was sick.

The diagnosis was ugly: a serious liver infection that was devouring his white blood cells. He was in and out of the hospital, and the last time I brought him in, he was too weak to walk. He was so thin and listless in my arms that I knew recovery was impossible. Everything that could be done for him had already been done.

As I walked back to my car, I was afraid that I would never see Trooper alive again. And I knew that I wasn't strong enough to take such a loss. But—did God realize that? Or did He think that I could survive *anything* because I had followed Him unquestioningly into so many difficult situations? I couldn't help it—I had to ask Him. Did He know how fragile I was? And how much I needed Trooper for a little while longer?

He did. He knew, He cared and He answered my need. Trooper recovered, to the astonishment of three veterinarians. He regained his weight and his jaunty manner, and he lived for two happy, dignified years—until I was strong enough to let him go.

And I learned what trust really is. I had been wrong to think that God expected me to follow Him blindly—and I'm sure that people like Samuel and Peter never did. God wanted me to follow *closely,* so that I could be safe. But I lagged behind or went in another direction because I thought God wouldn't want the company of someone with so many doubts and questions.

All along God knew how troubled I was. How hesitantly I followed. He knew how much strength I had left, and how much longer it would last. And He knew that I did not realize that He loved *me,* not my obedience. He loved *me,* doubts and all. It must have been very hard for Him to wait for me to trust Him. But He understood, better than I did, that questions are a normal part of life.

I still have questions about where we are going and what we are going to do when we get there. But I don't keep them to myself. I share them with God. Because that is what trust is: being completely open with Him. He is the only one who can answer these doubts we have about ourselves.

Why Can't We Do Things My Way?

It is very hard, almost impossible, for me to submit to anyone. Even to God. I like to make my own decisions, even if they aren't always right. I'm willing to pay for my mistakes. I'm always looking for advice, but I don't like to feel that I *have* to take it. I think I know what I want out of life, but I want the freedom to change my mind.

I don't want anyone telling me what to do, what to like or what to stop wanting. I want to set my own goals—I don't want someone else setting them for me. God gave me a mind and I want to use it. I can't turn it over to someone else. Not even to God.

But God doesn't want me to give up anything. He only

wants to show me how to make better use of the mind He gave me. That's what submission is: allowing God to show us how to use what we have to get what we need.

"Nobody tells me what to do," a friend of mine used to say. I have known Paul and his wife Elaine for many years. I know their two children: Carol, outgoing and achieving; and Bill—Bill is retarded. As a child, Bill was so lovable and easy to manage that the family discounted all the doctors' warnings. They kept Bill at home. Elaine was with him all day, every day, and Paul took over on evenings and weekends. Carol was an eager playmate. "From the moment Bill was born," Paul said, "all I wanted to do was love him. All I wanted God to do was *help* me love him."

By the time Bill was twelve, the family was exhausted. Bill was a big boy and not well coordinated. He broke things. He fell and hurt himself. The frustration he felt because he couldn't keep up with other children sent him into tearful rages. Reluctantly, the family agreed that Bill needed institutional care.

"Elaine and Carol took it better than I did," Paul said. "They thought Bill was doing well at the school we found. I disagreed. I kept imagining how he must feel, being away from his family, living with strangers." Paul brought Bill home almost every weekend. "It was rough," he says now. "Bill was always happy to see me, but when it was time to take him back to the school, he went into a tantrum. I'll never forget how rotten I felt, leaving him there. The doctors kept telling me not to take him home so often. They wanted me to give him a chance to make friends at the school. I was running into so much opposition that I wondered if God was sending me some kind of message. Was He trying to tell me to walk away and forget about Bill? I couldn't do that. I decided I didn't need that kind of help."

But Paul did need help. And he got it. Not the kind he wanted, and not in the way he wanted. He thinks he got something better.

At first, it didn't appear to be help at all. Private care for Bill was expensive, and Paul was running out of money. He was offended when Bill's doctor urged the family to allow the state to take over Bill's care. Bill functioned well enough, the doctor explained, to live in a group home with a small number of other patients and under supervision. He enjoyed doing simple, repetitive tasks and could handle a job. He might be happier that way, the doctor suggested. Paul didn't believe it—but he had no choice.

Bill went into a group home three years ago. He has his own room in a pleasant split-level house. He has his own television set. He goes to work five days a week in a van that picks him up and brings him home. He's very proud of earning his own way. On weekends he has a busy social schedule: swimming, bowling, bicycling, hiking and working in the yard. Occasionally he and his housemates go to a restaurant and a movie. He doesn't visit his parents often because he doesn't feel comfortable when he's away from "home." He misses his "family." But when his parents visit him, he's delighted to show them around. Bill *is* happy.

"He's more than happy," Paul says. "He's got independence and self-respect. That's what I always wanted for my son.

"I made it hard for God to help me love Bill—because I didn't understand how Bill had to be loved. I kept getting in his way, holding him back. Loving him meant getting *out* of his way—and that's what God was trying to tell me all along. He wasn't trying to change my mind—He was trying to open it."

Do I Have What It Takes?

I am like so many other disciples—unsure of myself. I'm afraid to go where I haven't been before, or to do something I've never done before. I'm afraid I'll discover that I just don't have what it takes.

Yet God seems to have so much confidence in me. He doesn't hesitate to put a challenge in my way, and He never has the slightest doubt that I can deal with it. I'm sure it would be easier for Him if I could take His word for it that I already have whatever I need to get along in this world. But sometimes He has to prove it to me. Sometimes I don't realize what He has given me until I have to use it.

Some years ago, when I was offered a managerial job with a small company, I was more excited than frightened. It was the right job at the right time, and I had the right amount of experience. I couldn't wait to begin. A year later I was asking God why He ever led me into such an unhappy situation: I had to fire someone.

Wendy was a departmental assistant, which meant she was part gofer, part typist and part file clerk. It was a demanding job, except that Wendy didn't see it that way. She was young and bored, so she invented reasons to avoid doing whatever didn't interest her. And the only things in the world that did interest her were motion pictures. She spent most of her days composing elaborate charts of movies and everything related to them—the casts, the directors, the technicians, the composers of background music, even the distribution dates. When anyone approached her desk, she quickly stuffed the charts into a drawer, but everyone knew what was going on. Wendy was such a gentle person, however, and so deeply committed to her movies that people forgave her her faults and found other ways to get their work done.

Wendy had been with the company for about two years when I came along, and it was made quite clear to me that I had to do something about her. I began by having a long talk with her. I thought we came to an understanding: she would pay more attention to her work, and do her charts on her own time. But Wendy didn't—or couldn't—change. Obviously I had to let her go.

I had been fired once, and I remembered how much it hurt. I could still see my boss coming out of his office and stopping by my desk to tell me he knew how hard I was trying, but I just wasn't right for the job. That's it—good-bye. He walked down the hall on his way to a meeting, and I sat there, fighting tears, panic and a sick feeling in my stomach. The man was absolutely correct—I was wrong for the job and no amount of effort could change that. But I felt as if someone had erased me.

How could I do that to anyone? I knew that it came with being a manager, but I began to wonder whether I was as qualified as I thought. I simply couldn't tear Wendy up and throw her away—could I? Or was God telling me that if I wanted to move up in the world, I had to be more practical?

Practical. The word stayed with me all the while I was making up my dismissal speech—which turned out to be only a few halting sentences to a very downcast Wendy. I knew she wasn't right for the job, but I couldn't stop believing that somewhere in this world there was a place for her. In a desperate effort to let her know that there was nothing wrong with *her,* I urged her to get a job where she could use her real talents.

"I don't have any," she said glumly.

"Yes, you do!" I told her. "Your charts!"

She was totally perplexed.

I hadn't realized until then how much knowledge and effort had gone into those charts. Wendy may have been a dud in our company, but when it came to motion pictures, she was an expert. A scholar. Surely there was a place for someone with so much savvy, I told her. Unfortunately I couldn't think of one, so I had to leave Wendy with her two weeks' notice and some words of encouragement. I told myself that it hurt me more than it hurt her, but I knew better.

A few months later I heard from Wendy again. Or, rather, from a man who was thinking of hiring her. He was the editor of a thriving local newspaper, and he was considering Wendy as a movie critic and columnist. She had given him my name as a reference; she told him I thought highly of her charts.

"I think they're wonderful!" Wendy's new boss said, as if I really didn't appreciate talent when I saw it. "We're going to run some of them in the weekend entertainment section."

Wendy never got in touch with me again. I think she couldn't quite forgive me for firing her. But I enjoyed reading her movie reviews and watching her become a local celebrity. She probably never knew it, but we had a lot in common: we both had doubts about ourselves. Wendy didn't think she had the kind of talent anyone wanted. And I didn't realize that I could be practical and still care. God had to prove to both of us that we were wrong.

Is God Still There?

It happens every time.

When I think I know where God is leading me, I start out so confidently. After all, what could possibly happen to me? But, along the way, my doubts creep in: Am I sure this is where God wants me to go? If it is, why am I running into obstacles? Why are things going wrong? Why aren't people returning my calls? Why are they changing their minds? Where is everybody? And, most important, where is God?

I know He's there, but I want more than His presence. I'm like a child. I want a word from Him, a signal, a gesture, something meant especially for me. I'm on the Emmaus Road, and I need reassurance for my anxiety. I need the touch of His spiritual hand on my all-too-human arm. I can get through the difficulties as long as I know He understands how I feel.

I want a booming voice, or the crack of thunder, a bright and shining light, waves parting before me, a mountain moving aside for me to pass. And that's not what I get. My reassurance comes in small, wonderful ways that only God would use, because He knows me so well.

Last year, for instance, about a week before my birthday I began to feel depressed. Would anyone remember the date? Would anyone send a card? What did all my years mean? What had I accomplished with my life? How much time was left? I went rummaging through all the mistakes I had made, wishing I had done something different. I wondered whether God thought I had wasted too many opportunities. I couldn't tell because He seemed so far away. My fault, not His. I had a bad case of middle-aged anxiety. I was afraid of getting old, and my fear was forming a barricade around me. No one could get through. Or so I thought.

When my birthday arrived, I almost didn't go to my mailbox, but when I did I found more cards than I've had since I was a schoolgirl. Even the friends who always forgot, remembered. And in the afternoon my neighbor's nine-year-old daughter, Robbi, came by with a friend to give me the card her whole family had signed.

"How did you know?" I asked her.

"Don't you remember?" she said. "I asked you last summer when your birthday was." I couldn't remember, but I was honored that she had wanted to know.

As the girls were leaving, Robbi turned to me with an apologetic smile and said, "My mom says I shouldn't ask this, but—how old are you?"

Ordinarily I don't try to conceal my age, but, looking at myself through the eyes of two nine-year-olds made me feel as ancient as Methusaleh. And, sure enough, when I told them, Robbi's friend gasped and covered her mouth with her hand. Robbi, however, reflected a moment, then looked up at me with a wholehearted smile. "You're not over the hill yet," she pronounced.

I was still laughing when I closed the door. Robbi had made my day. My *year*. She got through to me with something I had missed. The years didn't matter. Neither did the mistakes or the opportunities I had ignored. I had the gift of life, and God was reminding me that there was more of it ahead of me. What was I going to do with my next moment? And my next day? And all my days after that?

God had touched my arm and given me a little laughter to go along with the reassurance I needed so badly. It was a wonderful birthday.

How Long Can I Wait?

Sometimes, when I ask God for help, nothing happens. And that's scary. He never denies me, He never abandons me, but He has been known to make me wait a very long time for what I need.

Why?

Is He trying to teach me something? Is adversity somehow good for me? Will hardship, frustration and disappointment make me a better person? Does God want me to suffer? I can't believe that He does, for He has spared me a great deal of suffering during my life. And when I am trapped by life's cruelties, He seems to feel the pain even more than I do.

So, no, I don't think God is in favor of adversity. But He may be trying to show me how well equipped I am to deal with it.

Did I say that sometimes nothing happens when I ask for help? I was wrong. God gives me time, but I want action! What can I do with time?

Ever so much. I can learn more about myself.

If I'm alone and in need of friends, time allows me to find ways to *be* a friend. If a friend has hurt me, time allows me to remember how much that same friend has loved me. If I'm waiting for someone to keep a promise, time allows me to consider how I can do what I expect others to do for me.

In practical matters—if I am running low on money, time allows me to think of ways to stretch what I have left. If I'm under pressure to make a life-changing decision, time allows me to evaluate the consequences more carefully. If I'm getting anxious, time allows me to calm down. If I'm angry, time allows me to step back and get some perspective on the reasons for it. If I'm desperate, time allows me to discover how to be gentle with myself.

I don't mean that time itself solves our problems. But it gives us a chance to search ourselves for hidden resources. And even if we don't find what we need—even if we have to go back to God, again, for something we can't supply—we usually come away with something of value we didn't know we had.

When Ted came down with hepatitis, he took it personally. He was a doctor, and he should have known better than to push himself as hard as he did. No wonder he had no resistance. But a lot of people depended on him, and falling victim to an illness that requires a long period of inactivity was a mean trick for life to play on him.

Ted was the head of a geriatric department of a large urban hospital. The department was his idea and his baby. He was in on every part of it, from the blueprints stipulating the size of the rooms, to the placement and installation of every piece of equipment. He had a staff, a good one, but he couldn't help looking over their shoulders, tinkering with their ideas and suggesting revisions. He was in his office long before anyone else was in the building, and his wife complained that he stayed too late at night. He also refused to cut down on his case load; his patients needed him. What would they do now? What would happen to the department? Would it open on time? Ted hadn't finished selecting the staff—who would do that? Who would train them? Other doctors were involved in the project, but they didn't feel the way Ted felt about it. It wasn't their dream, their goal.

Ted tried to follow orders. He stayed in bed, he watched television and tried not to think about the work he wanted to finish. But he got worse. He prayed fervently for healing; his friends prayed for him. "I knew God hadn't abandoned me," he told me. "I knew He was doing something—but I couldn't see any results."

Nevertheless, something *was* happening. During the weeks and months of forced inactivity, during all the time Ted had to spend alone with himself, he began to see so many ways he could have avoided overexerting himself. He didn't have to do *everything*. And he didn't have to do everything *his* way. Some of the ideas he had overruled were better than his, and he just didn't want to admit it. Some of his patients needed more time than he could give to them, and they should have been under another doctor's care. Even the geriatric department was *not* his baby. It belonged to the people it was designed to help.

"That time I spent doing nothing may have been the best medicine in the world for me," Ted says. "It gave me a chance to come to terms with my pride. And once I did that, I began to recover. Oh, not in time to open the new department—the staff did that without me. And I have to admit that they did a great job. They even made a few improvements I hadn't thought of."

Thinking back, Ted shakes his head. "If God had healed me right away, which I wanted Him to do, I would have gone on and killed myself. But that time He gave me—well, I think it taught me how to live."

In spite of all the frustration it has brought Him, God did give us minds of our own, and He doesn't want them back. He wants, instead, a meeting of His mind and ours. A common view of where we are going and what is the best way for us to get there. A realization that God and we are in this world together.

God does not lead by walking ahead of us and urging us to catch up. He gets much closer than that. He becomes a part of us. He endures our human anxiety with us. He is compassionate toward our shortcomings and sensible toward our strengths. He will—if we will allow it—teach us how to live with them.

Trust is allowing God to get that close.

Chapter 3

— ❧ —

Speaking the Language
of God

BEFORE I MOVED TO the country, I lived for several years in a cottage that belonged in a fairy tale. It was on a small hill, sheltered by enormous trees that were planted around the turn of the century when the cottage was built. I had six tiny rooms. I felt as if I could wrap the house around me and snuggle down deep into it. My nearest neighbor on one side was a tiny stone church and a graveyard that went back a few centuries. On another side was a barn turned into an antiques shop, and a handsome house predating the Civil War. My neighbors and I were separated from each other by fields of grass that used to be a farm.

It was very quiet there. Secure. Until I had to leave the property.

About one hundred feet from my house was a four-lane road, and a quarter mile in any direction was a suburban sprawl of restaurants, hardware stores, gas stations and shopping malls. The traffic was heavy and fast, and getting out of my driveway was a hair-raising event. I tried every conceivable way to reduce the hazards of making a left turn, but finally I had to admit that going out into the world was a very dangerous business.

It always is, no matter where you live.

Nevertheless, I decided to move. I didn't want to risk my life just to get a bag of groceries.

Years ago, when my cottage was built, its owners were moving out from the city, and they must have felt the same way I did about the place they were leaving. At that time my busy street was a dirt lane, and people used a horse and wagon to get there. I'm sure that the couple who built my cottage felt they were moving to safety by leaving the city. But the world followed them out there. Just as it followed me when I moved farther away.

Wherever I am—and wherever you are—we will have to brave the world's dangers. Because we are needed there. And because we will find more of ourselves wherever we are needed.

When I am overwhelmed by life, I call on God for help. And I call on Him often. So I find it very hard to understand how I can be of use to Him. I have so many problems; how can I help others with theirs? I wasn't able to prevent the death of a friend. I don't know how to feed a starving child whose name I don't know. I see so much that is wrong in the world, but I don't know how to make it right. *I* have so many flaws. What does my voice mean when someone else's voice is louder? I can't even take back words I wish I had never said. Who am I to take on the woes of the world? Who are you?

We are the language of God. We are the means by which He communicates in the world. We are His way of saying, "I care." We are His love—in action.

There was a time when no barrier existed between God

and us. There was a time when words were pleasant, but not always necessary. We felt; God knew. God thought; we sensed. We lived so close to His power that we felt His strength as if it were our own. It was a time when we had no fear.

But it didn't last.

Being able to feel and to sense, we discovered that we and God were not alone in the world. And the sound of other voices was fascinating. Perhaps it was only curiosity that drew us toward them, but no matter. Before we knew it, the sounds grew loud and harsh, making it impossible for us to hear the voice of God. The silent conversation? Gone. The constant presence? No more. We were lost, with no sense of direction and no one to guide us.

In our confusion we sought hiding places. In our fear of being hurt, we hurt each other. We stole what belonged to others because—who would give to us? We lied—anything to be safe. Anything to avoid danger. We knew how fragile we had become. Without God, we didn't understand how to live in the world. We were afraid of it.

And the only way God could get through to us was to go into the midst of all the uproar and to speak in a voice we could recognize as both His—and ours. He became one of us.

It was a beautiful reunion, that moment when we recognized who Christ was. We hoped—we were *sure*—that now the other noises would go away. That once again we would know only the clear, strong voice of God in our ears. Once again we would feel His strength as if it were our own.

We were mistaken. God had not come to lead us out of the world but to teach us how to live in it. We watched Him do it. We witnessed His agony. We learned what it means to care. And we have never been the same.

How could we be? We have this part of God in us, and it is very different from what we are. Stronger, by far, yet also more willing to be hurt. Much more aware of imperfections, but more forgiving. More experienced in the ways of the world, yet still hopeful. And with a greater tolerance for frustration. We are the ones who expect miracles; God doesn't. We are the ones who want God to change the world; God waits for us to do it.

We try not to care. We're afraid to care. We don't want the pain. The misunderstanding. The unpopularity. The lack of appreciation. And the probability that caring doesn't accomplish anything.

Or does it?

Something to Give

So many times in my moments of need I have been helped by people who have known need themselves. I have a widowed friend who always seems to know the right moment to call me—because she knows how it is to be alone. When I am having a hard time putting my thoughts down on paper, a writer friend who knows how that feels can inspire me to keep trying. I'll never forget the friend who offered me money when I couldn't even tell anyone how desperately I needed it, and who was embarrassed by my gratitude. She knew what it was to be down to your last dollar. I have another friend who understands how hard it is, yet how necessary it is, to take a stand—and he has gone down fighting more than once.

I have been helped not only by friends, but by strangers,

too—like the man who ran the woodworking shop where I stopped to look at a pair of candlesticks a few years ago. He was big and gruff and impatient to get back to his carving. It was closing time and I was the last customer in the shop. I had difficulty deciding to buy the candlesticks because, beautiful though they were, something else had attracted my attention: a large photograph of a dog, of no recognizable breed, on top of an old desk in a corner. I was staring at it, smiling in the way you smile when you're trying not to cry.

Somehow that big, gruff, impatient man found the time and the gentleness to talk to me about the dog he had loved for so many years. And about his grief when the dog died.

If you have ever loved—and lost—an animal friend, then you know it is a special kind of grief. The relationship may have been very close, yet you can't talk to just anyone about how much you miss it because not everyone feels the same way about an animal. So your grief is very private, and your sorrow hurts all the more because it's hard for you to share it.

My own dog had died a few months earlier at the age of fifteen, and I missed him so much. Yet I found it difficult to talk about my grief without being told—with the best of intentions—that that's what happens when you get "attached" to a pet. But I knew that the man in the wood-working shop didn't feel that way. He had known the kind of loss I knew, and he understood. By recollecting about his own dog, he was giving me the assurance that I could talk about mine—which I did, for over an hour. And when I left the shop—entirely forgetting about the candlesticks—I knew the clench of grief was beginning to let go.

Because we have been given to, we are able to give. Because we have been helped, we are able to help someone else. Not that we are trying to pay back something we feel we owe. But rather that we have become more sensitive to the needs of others, even when they don't talk about them. We can hear what they're not saying—because the same words have gone through our own mind. We can feel the tension underneath a smile because we have smiled in that same stretched way.

You and I are much better equipped to brave the world than we realize. We may not be able to solve each other's problems, but we can give each other the patience and understanding we both need to go on living with them. We can't prevent death, but we can weep with the bereaved. We may not even *know* a starving child, but there are others who do, and we can learn how to get in touch with them. We may not be able to speak as loudly as the opposition when we see something wrong in the world—but the few people who hear us will know that there is another point of view.

You and I were created to take on the woes of the world. *That's* who we are. Human as we are, we have the strength of God in us. And, like Him, we will be hurt because we care. But, like Him, we will survive—and go on caring. Because it is in caring that we find the parts of ourselves that we thought we had lost.

So—getting back to why I moved to the country. . . .

It's quieter here. But I haven't escaped from the world. Because every time I encounter another person—someone new or an old friend—it's like making a left-hand turn into heavy traffic. There is a lot going on in other lives, and when they touch our own—which is what happens when we care—there is always the possibility of injury.

I can avoid that, if I choose. No one says I have to care.

No one says I have to try to change the world. God will love me just as much if I say No. But if I do say No, I will miss that surge of spiritual power going through me. God's voice will seem a little faint because I will not want to hear what He has to say.

I don't want to lose those parts of myself. I don't want to lose compassion, insight, appreciation, warmth, sensitivity —or even indignation and anger. These are the qualities that give my life meaning. These are some of the words that make up the language of God.

Being Loved

If you were to ask me to describe the voice of God, I couldn't do it. Yet I have heard His voice, many times. He doesn't speak the way you and I do. He doesn't use the same words. Sometimes He doesn't use words at all. I have heard Him speak through something a person does, through a smile, or a frown, or a wave of the hand—at the exact moment when I need those very things. I have heard Him speak through a song that comes unexpectedly to my lips for no reason other than to cheer me when I need cheering.

If there is one word to describe the language He uses, it is *love*. Which is why it is often hard for us to understand what God is saying: we don't know what love really is until we learn it from Him.

I thought I had to give something or do something in order to get love. I thought I had to be someone special— and if I didn't keep on being special, I would lose love. No offense intended, but I thought God only loved people who were worth loving—because that is the way *we* love.

Maybe it was because I wanted love so badly that I was a

well-behaved child. Some people spoil their children, but I spoiled my parents. They didn't have any problems with me—until I grew up and decided to get married. And, like many parents and children, we did not agree that I had made the right choice. My parents thought the young man was irresponsible; I thought they couldn't see his potential. They wanted us to wait until he finished his military service; we wanted to get married and help each other prepare for the future.

We planned a small informal wedding at the Church of the Transfiguration in Manhattan, better known as The Little Church Around the Corner. Dr. Randolph Ray, its celebrated pastor, was not free to perform the ceremony because we couldn't settle on a date far enough in advance. We never knew, until the last moment, when my husband-to-be would be granted leave. It was going to be a very spare ceremony because we didn't have enough money for flowers and organ music. We were saving every penny for our trip south to a Marine Corps base where we would live until my husband's enlistment time was up—or until he was sent overseas. I wasn't sure that my parents would even attend the wedding because they were so opposed to it.

I was not a typical happy bride. I was torn between my parents and the man I wanted to marry, and whatever I did I was going to hurt someone who meant a great deal to me. I felt so wrong that I didn't know how to ask God for help. I couldn't even believe He wanted anything to do with me.

I was working for a small trade association at the time, and on my last day of work my boss—a very demanding man and exceedingly penny-pinching—gave me a modest check as a wedding gift. Since I didn't expect anything at all, I felt rich! Immediately I called the church office and ordered flowers and organ music. Our ceremony wouldn't be so spare after all.

On the morning of my wedding, on the way to the church, I had a painful realization: I *was* making a mistake. Looking back, I know it was not too late to change our plans. But that wasn't the way I felt then. I didn't see how I could call off all the promises and arrangements we had made. I thought I was just panicky and would get over it.

At the church, I was surprised to see so many people in the chapel. It was a weekday morning, and some of our friends had taken time off from work to be there. My parents were there, and my stepfather wanted to walk me down the aisle. A very nice, elderly man I used to meet on the bus going to work was there. My doctor was there. So was my boss and some of the people from the office. And as the organist began to play and I looked toward the altar, I saw the minister take his place—and it was Dr. Ray, a tall, powerful-looking man with a deep sense of compassion about him.

It's very hard to describe how I felt—but I'll never forget it. I still knew I was making a mistake, and I still felt helpless to do anything about it. I didn't feel the least bit special or worth loving. *But I felt loved.* There was no way I could foresee what difficulties my weakness and poor judgment were going to bring to me—and there were many—but I knew I was not going to face them alone. God was as close to me as I would have hoped He would be if I had done everything right. He embraced me, He reassured me through the presence, the well-wishing and sweetness of others.

I had learned something about the language of God: it begins with Him loving us.

Loving Ourselves

I have trouble loving myself. I'm too conscious of my faults. How can I tell myself I'm wonderful when I know I'm not?

But that's not what love means. And we don't have to be wonderful in order to be loved—or to love ourselves. Loving ourselves means that we want to become the person God created us to be. But first we have to catch a glimpse of that person—through the eyes of others.

I was the child of a broken home, so I know what it is to live apologetically. Like many other children of broken homes, I felt responsible for the breakup. And when my father never came to see me, I was certain that there was something wrong with me: I was not lovable. Nothing, not the attention of my mother nor the compassion of my stepfather, could change that early conviction.

I tried to compensate for my unlovableness by being agreeable. Instead of learning what I needed to make my way in the world, I learned what other people needed from me and did my utmost to provide it. I didn't know how to receive, how to ask, how to lean. I didn't think I deserved such privileges.

When my own marriage broke up, it only seemed to confirm what I had thought all along. Yes, perhaps God could love me, but that was because He was God. Human beings are different. I didn't blame them. In fact, I agreed that I was unlovable. When I looked at myself objectively, all I saw were shortcomings.

All this I kept to myself because I hadn't developed the art of being close to anyone. I didn't want people to discover how unlovable I really was. Only God knew.

And then two small events occurred: someone prayed, and someone wept. Someone asked God to lift my despair, and someone felt my pain so intensely that the tears came. I have never been the same since—because my eyes have been opened to a different view of myself.

I have learned how to love myself through seeing the unmistakable signs of love in the eyes of others. They were there all along, but I didn't know what to look for.

Now, when I see encouragement, I know it doesn't mean I have to win first prize; I just have to try to be me. When I see compassion, I know it isn't pity; it's a willingness to share my downs as well as my ups, and you can't get a better relationship than that. When I see a frown, I know it doesn't mean I've done something wrong; it may mean that someone is having a little difficulty getting through my defenses. A smile isn't making fun of me; it's enjoying me.

I can look back now and see that there was no reason for me to apologize for being here. I was created by a loving God who felt that I had something to bring to His world. I was not created to bring people together—or to drive them apart. I was not meant to supply what is missing from someone else's life. There are many wonderful things that I am not, and never will be, but I have my share of worthwhile qualities. I am honest, I try to be fair, and I care. What happens to you is important to me. I may not be able to make your dreams come true, but I will do everything I can to help you become the person you can be.

I guess you could say that I am beginning to see who I really am. And, with God's help, who I can become. That's what it means to love ourselves. It is our first opportunity to speak the language of God, our first attempt to give His love to someone else. So it makes sense to practice on ourselves.

Loving Each Other

I know I have faults, but I'm always surprised when people I love have them. For some reason I expect people I love to be perfect, and when I find out that they aren't, I'm uncomfortable. I begin to wonder if I made a mistake to love them in the first place. And then I realize that love—God's kind of love—is often uncomfortable. Because it hurts.

Recently I was badly shaken to discover that a friend I've known for many years is greedy. He will give you the shirt off his back, but he wants you to return it the next day. If you need more than his shirt, you're in trouble. And if you want to do business with him, be prepared to fight over every dollar.

Another friend is manipulative. When she doesn't want to do something, she gets sick—and recovers as soon as you agree to do things her way. A very dear couple overprotect their grown children and nibble away at their self-confidence. A woman I admire for her intelligence is a fool about men. One of the sweetest men I know is also the most narrow-minded.

I'm not bad-mouthing these friends of mine. I'm not saying that my faults aren't as big or as bad as theirs. But I'm trying to understand how we can go on loving each other. Because the human kind of love I'm accustomed to can't put up with such faults. Obviously, God can.

How?

How did Christ put up with His disciples? Along with everything He loved about them, He saw their envy, their pettiness, their hypocrisy, their greed, their pushing and shoving and manipulating. They weren't always dependable, and they were more than eager to take the easy way out.

Why didn't He try to change them? *How* did He go on loving them?

By allowing Himself to be crucified. By suffering, in their place, for all their faults. He paid the price for all the things they did wrong—instead of making them pay. And if we want to go on loving each other, after we discover how imperfect we all are, we have to be willing to take some pain.

If I want to go on loving the people I love, then I have to be willing to suffer the pain of disappointment, frustration, sadness and even anger along with the kindness, thoughtfulness, generosity, devotion, gentleness, and all the other blessings they bring to my life. I cannot change them. I cannot insist that they change themselves. I have to love them the way God does—the way they are. And sometimes that will be uncomfortable.

If it is so hard, sometimes, to go on loving the people I love, how can I love a stranger? Especially one I dislike?

I will have to suffer a little more pain.

I have already come so far in learning the language of God that I have forgotten where I began. Remember? *I* thought *I* was unlovable. And perhaps, to many people, I am. But that is because they haven't seen what God put into me. So, when I find someone utterly abhorrent, I am not seeing what God originally created that person to be.

Speaking the language of God doesn't mean I can excuse what a person does. But I can love what a person is.

I know someone who wants me for a friend, but I find it hard to be one. He leans on me—too much. He has not had a good life. At a very young age he was denied love and care. He was ridiculed when he desperately needed encouragement, ignored when he needed understanding. Now, in his middle years, he wants others to make up for all the neglect.

And he lashes out at anyone who will not comfort him. He calls people at all hours and demands that we drop our own concerns and take on his. He invents emergencies that bring us running, and then he blames us for not running fast enough. He drinks too much and denies it. His remorse over his abuses is so agonizing that we feel responsible for it—until we come to our senses.

But I see something else in this man. I see someone capable of caring deeply, someone with a quick mind and a generous spirit. Someone who could grow into the protector and friend he is seeking in others. He could *be* a good friend—if only . . .

I cannot love what this man does. I cannot be the kind of friend he wants. But I find that I can love the *if only* in him, the part of him that God created—the rest is what the world added on.

That feeling of love comes over me so powerfully at times that I pick up the phone and call him just to say hello, even though I know I will suffer the pain of his complaint that I don't call often enough. I spend part of a day with him and truly look forward to it, even though I know my enthusiasm will be crushed by his bitter attacks on anything I value. When he has had too much to drink and calls to vent his anger on me, I can't bring myself to hang up. But because I have learned to love myself, I can't listen. I put the phone down on the table and walk away, but there are tears in my eyes.

I am new to the language of God, so I speak it haltingly. But I am beginning to understand what it means. It says, "I love you—the way God loves me." Some people call it forgiveness.

Chapter 4

—— 🙢 ——

Of Course I Can—I Think

DON'T BE FOOLED BY APPEARANCES.

If you had seen me trying to get a job on a newspaper when I was fresh out of college, you might have assumed I was full of confidence. That's the impression I wanted to make, and I succeeded.

I did everything my college job counselor told me to do. My resume was beautifully typed. My clothes were appropriate. And I made an appointment to see the newspaper's publisher. No personnel department for me!

It was a small daily newspaper in a small southern town. The publisher was not especially busy, which may have been the reason I got the appointment. But I think I got the job because the poor man didn't know what else to do with such a serious young woman who not only asked if a job was available, but how far I could go in it, how much money I would make, when I would make more, and what the fringe benefits were.

Offering me a job—and there *was* one available—may have been the only polite way the publisher could get me out of his office. And he was a man known for being mannerly. Of course, I couldn't see that at the time. I was stunned by the offer of the job, and I took it. My job counselor was right: "Act confident, even if you're not. That's how you get to *be* confident."

Getting the job, however, did not make me confident. It made me very uneasy. I didn't feel like the person I was trying to be. I had learned what a reporter is supposed to do. But I had never done it. When I came up against someone who didn't want to give me information, I didn't know what to do. When I interviewed someone who had difficulty putting thoughts into words, I didn't know what other kinds of questions to ask. And when I returned to my desk at deadline time with excuses instead of news, my editor left me nothing to be confident about. He didn't have to tell me: I was on probation.

I blamed my predicament on a lack of confidence. Following the advice of my job counselor again, I put all my energies into persuading myself that I could, indeed, do the job. Three other reporters, whose desks surrounded mine, were busy tapping away at their typewriters. Why couldn't I?

Because self-confidence is not insisting "I can!" It's asking *"Can* I?" It's not Peter vowing he will give his life for his Lord. It's Peter knowing very well that in a crunch he will try to save his own neck. Self-confidence is the ability to be open to the truth about who we really are.

As a reporter I was anything but self-confident. I was a newcomer in a small town in a part of the country where I had never been. I didn't know anyone. I didn't know the customs, the way people spoke or the way they thought. I didn't even know my way around town and was constantly getting lost. I was scared, and couldn't admit it—because that would mean I wasn't self-confident.

Oh, no, it wouldn't! I didn't realize it then, but I was confusing self-confidence with arrogance. Many of us do.

Arrogance always seems to know what it is doing, where it is going, and how to get there. And this is what we like to think self-confidence is. But look a little closer.

Arrogance is the one who says, "Yes, I can!" without ever considering the possibility that maybe it can't. Or that maybe it will have to find a different way to do what must be done. Or that maybe it will need more time, more help, more preparation. What arrogance wants is what counts. It gives no thought to consequences—to others or to itself. It is insensitive to its own feelings or to those of anyone else. It is determined, stubborn, resentful of opposition, and learns nothing from its mistakes. It can—and often does—bring its own house down upon its head. It can become a great success or a dismal failure and never know why—because it never gets to know the self that God created. It knows only the role it is trying to play. It will not look within itself because it thinks nothing is there. Arrogance is the man who believes he can run the business better than his boss can—and proves it by going into business for himself. But it is also the pitcher who insists he can still play even though his good stuff is gone.

Self-confidence, on the other hand, asks a lot of questions: Is this something I can do? Is this the right way to get there? Do I really want it? Should I try again? What will happen? It looks at life through a wide-angle lens and sees more than the road ahead. It sees obstacles, reactions, effects and, most important, consequences. It can't always walk in a straight line to where it wants to go—it takes detours, backtracks, sometimes even goes in circles, depending on what it meets along the way. Because what it meets along the way gives it a chance to learn more about itself. And that is very important. Self-confidence is the conviction that God has put much more into us than we have had time to bring out. Self-confidence is Peter discovering that even though he didn't have enough courage to give his life, he had enough devotion to do it.

When I thought I was going to lose my job, I hoped God would help me to find another one. He didn't. He helped me to hold onto the one I had.

I think my editor wanted to get me off my regular beat because I wasn't bringing back much news from it. So, on the spur of the moment, he assigned me to interview a young woman who had won the title "Queen for a Day" on a popular radio show. She and her husband were in town to take part in our local parade and spring festival. It was a run-of-the-mill interview and one that I knew would probably get scrapped in favor of more interesting news. I was on my way out.

As I walked the few blocks to the motel where the couple was staying, I couldn't think of any questions to ask them. Certainly not "How does it feel to be Queen for a Day?"—and there didn't seem to be anything else I could say. I was tired of trying to behave like a reporter when obviously I wasn't one. I decided I wouldn't even use the steno-pad in my pocketbook. There wouldn't be any need for notes.

The couple was very young and very thrilled. Two years earlier, when they were married, they couldn't afford a honeymoon, so the trip to our festival was making up for what they had missed. They were so excited and so grateful that I forgot about my own distress and just enjoyed being in their company. I wasn't interested in getting information; I was interested in two nice people. If this was to be my last day on my job, it was turning out to be the first good one.

It was while Queen for a Day was unpacking the new wardrobe she had won that she mentioned how foolish she felt because she had forgotten to bring the ballgown, the one she was to wear in the parade. She held up a pretty print dress and asked me if I thought that would do. No, I said, it wouldn't, and she looked so unhappy that I couldn't stand it. I found a telephone book and began going through the Yellow Pages. It took three calls for me to find a dress shop that carried evening gowns. I asked for the owner and explained why a gown was needed. She graciously offered one as a gift.

When I returned to my typewriter I realized that I had a story to write. But at least it *was* a story. Maybe my editor would find space for it on page ten or eleven.

The story, along with a photograph of the Queen in her lovely new gown, made page one, and I got a byline. It was also picked up by a wire service, which pleased my editor. "I'm keeping you on feature stories," he said. "You're no good at news."

I'll never know whether he was right, because I went on writing feature stories. But perhaps by then I could have written straight news just as well. The reason I was able to write *anything* was that I stopped trying to be a reporter. I began, instead, to be the person God was helping me to discover—a scared, inexperienced newcomer who was more comfortable listening to people than asking them questions.

With all due respect to my former job counselor, I have to disagree. The way to become confident is *not* to act confident. That's arrogance. That's going it alone. The way to become confident is to face up to our doubts. Because, very often, finding out what we can't do leads us to what we can do.

Self-doubt is not the evil ogre we have been taught to believe it is. It's an honest attempt to answer some very important questions.

What Do I Really Want to Do?

When I was a child, there were several things I wanted to do when I grew up: be a veterinarian, be a writer, be a dancer, or be an actress. The veterinarian and writer fantasies were mine; my mother visualized me on the stage. I gave up the idea of being a veterinarian almost immediately because as much as I loved animals, I fell apart when I saw one suffer. I began writing when I was very young, but I knew that publication was a long way off. Nevertheless, the work itself pleased me, and I had an endless amount of patience.

Dancing and acting were something else. Even though my mother encouraged me, I hated to go onstage. Perhaps that is why I never got the lead in a play. I tried out for Snow White and got the part of the Wicked Stepmother. I wanted to be the diabolical young woman in *Guest in the House,* and played the stalwart wife instead. I was the understudy for the glorious-voiced ingenue in our senior play, which somewhat amazing since I had a thin, wavering voice. I got nowhere in our neighborhood dance studio, and dropped out after less than a year. I decided that I wasn't meant for a life on the stage—I couldn't handle so much disappointment.

Meanwhile, I was handling my disappointments as a writer very well. Rejections meant nothing to me. I simply addressed a new manila envelope and sent my stories off to someone else.

Do you see what I am getting at? When we're going in a direction that is right for us, we can take the opposition we meet along the way. But when we're trying to do something we don't want to do, we are easily defeated. It's not a mystery. When we love what we do, that love gives us the strength to put up with the stress of obstacles, frustrations, delays and things we just don't like to do.

Scott was a young minister who was trying very hard to follow in his well-known father's footsteps, and not succeeding. As a preacher, he showed some promise, but there is more to being a minister than the Sunday sermon. Even though his congregation was small, Scott was overwhelmed with all the administrative responsibilities he had. He dreaded the Official Board meetings with their dire reports of repairs to the grounds and buildings, and the growing shortage of Sunday school teachers, and the fierce debates over reducing the mortgage. He couldn't remember his father agonizing over such things, yet *his* church had been enormous by comparison. His father never found it difficult to urge parishioners to support their church, but Scott got tongue-tied asking for money.

He knew the Official Board would not put up with him much longer, so he tried harder to be more effective. The result was that one Sunday morning, in the middle of his sermon, he burst into tears and had to be helped from the pulpit.

Later that afternoon he lay staring up at the pattern of window light on his bedroom ceiling, wondering why he had failed in something he wanted so much. As he reached for the pitcher of water on his nightstand, his hand brushed the wooden decoy that always rested there. It was a beautiful replica of a black duck he had made as a teenager, and he had kept it with him all these years. The satiny smoothness of the wood was soothing to his touch, and as he picked it up he remembered how his hands always used to feel when he worked with wood. They felt strong, capable, as if they could do anything he wanted them to do. Back home, locked away in the attic of his widowed mother's house, were all the other beautiful things he had done with wood. More decoys, meticulous in detail and color, large chests of glowing cherry and cedar cut from trees that grew in the woods behind the house. He remembered selecting the trees and then waiting for them to season before taking them to the sawmill. He spent hours—days, sometimes—planing the boards. Then he sawed them lovingly and watched them give shape to an idea that, until then, had only existed in his mind.

Lovingly—that's what was missing from his ministry, and it had made all the difference. His father had not only preached but administered lovingly—he felt the way Scott felt when he worked with wood: strong, capable, able to turn a thought or an idea into something people could see and touch and use.

It took courage for Scott to write his letter of resignation to the Board that evening. He also realized that his father, were he still alive, might be disappointed in a son who wanted to be a woodworker. But he thinks now that his father would understand and approve of a son who was honest with himself.

What Did I Do Wrong?

I'm very proud of the way my dog Kate behaves—and I should be. She and I worked with a trainer for more than a year on basic obedience, so that now, when I say something, Kate knows exactly what I expect of her. It has paid off in many ways, the most important one being the wonderful communication Kate and I have with each other. We really are the best of friends.

One day, however, when I took Kate walking in a nearby park, we were approached by a young woman who was jogging along the path with her dog. Kate was on a lead and the other dog wasn't, but Kate is usually friendly and the other dog seemed to be. Suddenly, just as the dogs were passing each other, the other dog made a lunge at Kate and dashed off—and Kate responded by dashing after her, with me on the other end of the lead. I held on and was pulled down and dragged in the dirt before Kate came to a stop.

I was furious. I saw blood on my knees and on one elbow, but I felt no pain. As I sat up, with Kate licking my face, the woman walked back toward me, murmuring words of concern. I cut her off. "How can you walk that dog off lead when you don't have any control over her?" I roared.

"But she didn't mean any harm," she explained.

"How do *you* know? How am I supposed to know?" I demanded.

The poor woman began to back away. "I'd like to help you," she said, "but I'm afraid to come near you—you're so angry."

By then we had attracted a few onlookers, so I got up and continued on my walk with Kate, too proud to give in to my wounds, muttering about how irresponsible some people are.

I wish now that I could find that woman and apologize to her. Because I was as irresponsible as she was. Maybe she didn't know how to control her dog, but I did—and I was not in control of Kate. A simple command, properly spoken, would have stopped Kate in her headlong chase and I wouldn't have been pulled down. In my surprise, I simply forgot to say the right word, which is no excuse when you've had all the training Kate and I have had.

I remember the incident for another reason. It took a little while, but I finally admitted to myself that I had been wrong—and the sky didn't fall in. In fact, I think both Kate and I have been behaving better ever since. Maybe we learned something from our mistakes.

Do I Need Help?

A friend of mine is having family problems. But when I suggest that she see a counselor or a therapist, or perhaps join a support group, she refuses. "That would be an admission of weakness," she says. I don't know how to respond to her because, in a way, I suffer from the same misconception.

I like to do things for myself. I don't like to ask for favors or to impose on people. Why? Because I don't want to accept the possibility that I have limitations. I want to be able to do anything.

And yet I can't.

Last summer I ordered some gravel for my driveway,

and when it had been deposited all the way from the road to my garage door, there was still some left in the truck.

"Where would you like me to dump this?" the driver asked.

I told him to dump it right there in the large turning area outside the garage. "I'll spread it around with a rake," I said.

"You sure?" he said. "It's pretty heavy stuff."

I was not about to be told that I wasn't strong enough to spread a little gravel. "I can handle it," I told him. That was before he emptied the truck.

I was left with a pile of gravel eight feet high and twelve feet square, so close to the garage that I couldn't get my car out. It was noontime, July, and getting hotter by the minute. I estimated that I could finish in an hour.

The moment I swung my metal rake into the gravel, I realized why the driver had such doubt in his eyes. I had never worked with gravel and had no idea how heavy it is. My rake bounced off the surface and my shoulder vibrated from the impact. A few stones rattled to the ground.

An hour later I was standing on top of my rock pile, shoveling gravel into a wheelbarrow. I had filled the wheelbarrow several times and dumped the contents somewhere else in the driveway, and, as far as I could see, I hadn't reduced the pile at all. The heat was getting to me and so was my anger at my stubbornness.

I went into the house to cool off, get a drink of water, and to consider whether I should call the gravel supplier and beg—I mean it, *beg!*—him to send the truck back. I had already picked up the phone when I heard a loud, scraping noise outside. It was my neighbor from the farm across the road, a woman I had met once and waved at from a distance.

She and her daughter were spreading my gravel with a huge tractor fitted with a snowplow blade. Over the noise she said, "I hope you don't mind, but this is a much faster way to do it!" I could have cried.

In fifteen minutes, my mountain of stone was gone and some of my foolishness along with it. I was all wrong about weakness and limitations and independence.

I am weak when I refuse to use someone else's strength. I am limited when I try to do everything my way. I am independent only as long as someone else is there in case of need.

I still like to do things for myself, but when I can't I know that God isn't telling me to give up. He's telling me to get help—because that's what strong people do.

When Should I Give Up?

I don't think of myself as persistent. I'm too realistic. If a plan doesn't seem to be working out, I look for a better one. I don't try to force dreams to come true.

Nevertheless, some of my dreams have been with me for a long time. Even though they keep meeting with failure, they don't go away. They just seem to wait around.

For instance, when I was a child I always wanted to live in the country. I never went to the country for more than a short drive on the way to somewhere else, but I felt good being there. I thought I might live there when I grew up, but I couldn't. I had to live within commuting distance of a city. So I gave up the dream—I thought. Even when I worked in an office in my home, I didn't think of moving until an unexpected opportunity came my way. I was looking for a house, and the only one I could afford was in a beautiful country valley. The childhood dream came back.

On the day I moved, I began to get nervous. Looking in the rearview mirror at the moving van following me, I realized that I really didn't know anything about my new home. I hardly knew how to get there. The houses were farther apart then they are in the suburbs. I hadn't met my neighbors. I didn't know where the nearest store was. Or the nearest gas station. At night there would be no street lights—would I be afraid of the darkness? There weren't any fire hydrants—the nearest firehouse was one-and-a-half miles away. I had a well—I knew nothing about a well.

That first night, after the movers left, I was surrounded by boxes I was too tired to open. I made up my bed and climbed in. It was winter, and the silence was noticeable. No crickets or frogs. No voices or sounds from other houses. And absolutely no traffic. I had never known such a peaceful environment.

The next morning I was awakened by birds who insisted that I get up. But I like to get up early, so I felt at home.

I felt *very much* at home—not only with the sound of birds and the evening silence, but with the country itself. As I scouted through boxes to find my coffee pot and a few plates for my breakfast, I had the feeling that I belonged there. The house was new to me; I hadn't had time to probe its corners, become familiar with its sounds, and find my way around in the dark, but it was as comfortable as if it had been mine all my life. I could see so many trees outside my windows, but I couldn't identify any of them without my copy of *An Instant Guide to Trees*—and that would have to wait until spring when the leaves blossomed. But it was good having so many trees around me, almost as if I had been missing them all those other years.

No, I would not be lonely in the country. I would find my way around. I would make new friends. I was already finding a part of myself I didn't know existed. A part of me that had gone to live there when I was a little girl and had a dream that took a while to come true.

So I have a very high regard for dreams that refuse to go away. Which is why I could understand why my friend Rebecca went to college at the age of fifty-five.

"What on earth for?" her husband Gus asked, because he was considering his company's offer of an early retirement.

"Well, I've always wanted to do it," Rebecca said. And Gus, remembering, understood why.

Rebecca had always wanted to go to college, but something always got in her way. First it was a lack of money, so Rebecca got a job right after graduating from high school and saved every penny she could. But then she met Gus, who was already in college. When he graduated, they got married and Rebecca's job helped him get through graduate school. Once Gus was on his way, they began having children, and before Rebecca knew it, she was too old to go to school.

Or was she? According to her son David, a teacher, his best students were Rebecca's age. He said they had a serious desire to learn.

So Rebecca enrolled, and Gus chewed his nails down, hoping she wouldn't be in for a disappointment. For a long time, Rebecca was ready to give up after each class. She had forgotten how to study, how to exclude from her mind all the other big and little demands of her life and just concentrate on her goal. She felt tacky, selfish and silly. But she kept at it because something in her felt satisfied: her mind was challenged.

Rebecca got her degree the same year Gus retired. She'd like to continue her education and become a Certified Public Accountant, but she'll do that part-time, because Gus wants to travel. She knows she's too old to think of a career as an accountant. But she wants something else. "I want to know I can do something that I always wanted to do," she says. "It's a part of myself that I have to be."

Chapter 5

— ❧ —

At Home in the World

SOME PEOPLE WERE IMPRESSED by her courage. Some called her a fool.

At the age of thirty-nine she was giving up a well-paying job as a hospital administrator and going back to school—to study art history. "My family thinks I'm crazy," she told me. "And maybe I am—but I have to find out."

Ever since childhood Ruth was interested in art—not as an artist but as a scholar. "A museum is like home to me," she said. But since curator jobs are hard to come by, Ruth thought it made more sense to aim for a business career. After three degrees and several years of hard work, she wasn't getting any satisfaction out of what she was doing. There was still that feeling, every time she walked into a museum, that this was where she belonged.

Ruth's decision meant giving up some things that were important to her. She enjoyed having her own apartment, but she knew she wouldn't be able to afford it. She planned to move in with a friend. She needed a new car, but that would have to wait. Her savings would go toward her tuition. And, of course, there was the realization that she might be making a mistake. "It's a risk I have to take," she said.

It's a risk each of us will have to take, at some point in life, as we discover more about ourselves. It is the point at which we stop doing what seems to make sense and listen instead to the voice of God. The risky part is that we may be misunderstood. Those who care about us may stop believing in us. With the very best of intentions, they may try to cajole, persuade, command and even belittle us into giving up our attempt to bring out into the world what we know is inside of us. They will measure our progress against their own standards of success and failure—and we know very well what they are because we used to live by them too.

We will fantasize a little. We will look forward to the day when all our doubters will have to admit that we were right. We knew what we were doing. We succeeded. But such a day may never come, because our success—and we will have it—may not be seen as success by anyone else. Except God.

Success Story

"It didn't even look like a risk, at first," Tony said, describing the case that almost finished him as a lawyer. He had gone through the lean years and his practice was beginning to show a profit. He and his family had moved to a house in the suburbs—nothing elaborate, just comfortable. Like many young lawyers who want to gain experience, Tony had occasionally served as a public defender for people who were accused of a crime and couldn't afford an attorney. He didn't pick his cases; he was assigned to them by the court. He had one more case to go, and then he was taking his name off the list. "I couldn't afford to work for nothing anymore," Tony quipped. "That's what success does to you."

He was assigned to represent a young man named Ben who was accused of firebombing a neighbor's house and causing the death of a woman and a child. Ben claimed that he couldn't remember much about the night of the fire. He had gone out with a few friends. They had a couple of drinks and Ben blacked out. Had that ever happened before? Tony asked. No.

"What got to me," Tony said, "was his own doubt. He kept saying, 'Do you think I could have done such a thing?' He wasn't even trying to defend himself—if he did it, he wanted to be punished for it. I don't come up against that very often."

As he looked into the background of the case, Tony came across some other disturbing facts. Ben had been arrested after an anonymous tip to the police. He was identified as one of three young men who were seen sitting in a car across the street from the house that was later set on fire, but no attempt had been made to identify the other two men. Ben also had some bruises on his face when Tony first saw him. Had he been roughed up during his interrogation? Ben changed the subject. "The kid was scared," Tony said.

The prosecutor's office was less than cooperative. The firebombed house was in a neighborhood vibrating with racial tensions, and the prosecutors wanted the case settled quickly. As far as they were concerned, they had their man. They were in a hurry to go to trial.

"I could understand how they felt," Tony said. "They had other crimes—worse ones—to try. To them, Ben was just a punk with a mean temper, so why not put him away? I always got along well with them before, so they were trying to tell me not to waste my time."

And it might be a waste of time, Tony knew that. He could, in good conscience, try to get Ben off with a lighter sentence and be quite certain of success. Or he could try to do the impossible—find the evidence to prove Ben's innocence—and maybe lose the case. He wasn't a trained detective; he would have to hire one and pay for it out of his own pocket.

Did Ben mean that much to him? And was he that convinced of Ben's innocence? The answer to both questions was Yes. "He wasn't a punk," Tony said. "He was a good kid. Not the brightest kid in the world and he didn't have much education. But he didn't deserve to go to jail because of what he didn't have—and what he didn't do." Tony decided to try to prove Ben's innocence.

He didn't realize how much it was going to cost him until six months later. His practice suffered because he didn't have time for much more than Ben's case. And some of his more discriminating clients were uncomfortable with an attorney who was getting so much attention from the press. "I couldn't blame them," Tony said. "If you read the newspapers, you'd think I was a crackpot." Some of his fellow attorneys apparently agreed with that interpretation: they avoided him at lunch and stopped referring cases to him. One retired judge reminded him that it wasn't a good idea to get on the wrong side of the city administration.

Tony lost the case. He had presented the possibility that two of Ben's friends had firebombed the house and deliberately implicated him. But he didn't have the evidence he needed to convince a jury. He needed more time. He asked for an appeal.

That night Tony's wife looked at him silently for a long time, and then she asked, "Are you sure you're right?" And Tony answered, "No—but I have to find out." He knew as well as his wife did that they could no longer keep the house in the suburbs. And he wondered how many more sacrifices his family would be willing to make for him. "It was harder for them," he said. "They didn't have that voice inside them saying, 'Go ahead—don't give up.' There were times when I wished I didn't have it, either."

It took four more months for Tony to get the evidence he needed to prove that Ben's two friends had drugged him, committed the crime, and led the police to him. He was also able to prove that Ben had been improperly treated during his arrest and interrogation. The charges against Ben were dropped and he was a free man. The day he was released, Tony was the only one there to meet him. Even the press had lost interest in the case.

Now, a few years later, Tony has rebuilt his practice, but it won't ever be what it was. He didn't take his name off the list of public defenders, and he handles a few other cases that aren't exactly profitable. He misses the house in the suburbs, but, as he says, "Some things are more important—like seeing that kid go free. That was the day I discovered what I wanted to do with my life."

Success, as we once knew it, was an award for outstanding achievement, a signal that the hardest times were behind us. To God it means picking up whatever belongings we can carry and setting out across a desert for a land we only *think* is there. Success used to mean that we didn't fail. To God it means getting up and going on no matter how many times we fall down. Success used to be the sound of applause. Now we know it means an inner voice that no one else can hear. Success used to be visible—in the way a person dressed, where a person lived, what a person owned. Now we know it is something we can feel: success is being at home in the world.

Where Do I Fit In?

In the distance, from my window, I can see a thick column of white steam rising above the hills. It masquerades as a cloud, but everyone in the valley knows it isn't. It is the vapor from a nuclear power system twenty miles away. We are told that the vapor is harmless and we know that the system lights and heats thousands of homes, but every time they test the screeching warning signals, we wish there were some other way. So many people say they never wanted the system, yet here it is.

I want to be well informed, so I read two news magazines, two newspapers, and I listen to a news program first thing in the morning and the last thing at night. But I don't like the information I am getting: leaders with power over my life are destroying their own, men and women are insisting that it's all right to tell lies, people are being cheered for doing something wrong.

I don't like what I see, either: bars on windows, and burglar alarms, a commuter sniffing something behind a newspaper on the morning train, kids walking with that hesitant, where-did-the-sidewalk-go? step that tells you they're on something—and the homeless, the ones you see and the ones who are too weak to come out and scavenge through your trash.

I see so much greed, self-centeredness and corruption that I wonder, How can I be at home in a world like this?

By looking at it through the eyes of God, because He sees what we overlook.

Our world is not so different from the world Christ entered as a Man. He saw irresponsible leaders. He saw the poor robbed of what little they had. He heard the lies people told each other. He knew what it was to walk down a dark street alone at night. Very often He was homeless and hungry. He saw fingers pointed and heard the names they called Him. Even some of His friends deserted Him.

But He saw something else in the world. He saw the love in it. He saw an old woman give away a coin she needed for herself. He saw a boy share his food with all comers. He saw the exuberance of a family celebrating a wedding. He saw the love of a mother for a stricken child. He saw the regard of a Roman soldier for the faith of his slave. He saw the courage of men and women who left their familiar world to share His dangerous one.

Why can't I see these things? Because I'm looking at the world with contempt for all that is wrong with it—and the dark color of my contempt filters out all that is right.

Christ knew what was wrong with the world. That's why He came. But He looked upon it with love, and love illuminates what is good.

I can do the same thing by looking at the world through the eyes of God. I will not be spared any of the world's ugliness. But I will see much more. I'll see that next door to my house—facing the column of steam on the opposite horizon—is a bird sanctuary. It's part of a county park surrounding a large reservoir where, even at night, you can hear the sounds of migrant and resident birds whose existence is unthreatened. It's not a perfect spot; there are evidences of pollution. But a small group of people who love the land are working very hard to clean it up. And they are succeeding. I feel at home with them.

Not all leaders abuse their power. One of my neighbors is the chief of our volunteer fire department. He wears a beeper on his belt, and sometimes in the middle of the night I hear him driving down the road to help someone. I know a juvenile court judge who puts her free time into persuading kids in trouble to stay in school. The postmaster of a big city branch spends a lot of time at AA, working with new members. He carries a blue chip in his pocket—sometimes in his hand. It represents twenty years without a drink, his proudest achievement. A young woman just out of college feels she really accomplished something because she helped a friend break a cocaine habit. And one of my friends with bars on her windows gently captures a cricket in a paper cup and releases it outside for a second chance at life. I am finding a home among these people. They are teaching me to look at the world with love.

Christ was right. Corruption, greed and self-centeredness are the losers in this world. The winners are morality, sacrifice and compassion.

Is Anybody Honest?

Recently I had to face the fact that I had been corrupted. No, I didn't lie, cheat, steal, accept a bribe or break a law. But I refused to believe that someone was innocent even when a jury did. I didn't know the man; I read about him in the newspapers. He owned a construction company and was accused of seeking political favors to get a valuable piece of property rezoned. When he was acquitted, I thought, "Oh, sure, somebody bought off somebody." And then I realized what was happening. I had been corrupted by corruption! I saw it everywhere. Because some people were corrupt, *everyone* was corrupt. I couldn't accept the possibility that morality still exists. But it does.

My friend Barry is a salesman with a long record of safe driving, but one day when he was going down a narrow city street, a little boy ran out in front of his car. Barry stopped, but not in time to avoid hitting the boy. The child appeared to be bruised and stunned, but otherwise all right. Just to be sure, he was taken to the hospital.

Barry kept calling the hospital every half hour to find out how the child was, and when he learned that the boy was fine, he cried with relief. "I never want to hurt anyone," he said. "I couldn't live with that."

Then Barry began to make plans. The boy had never been to a baseball game—Barry would take him to one. He'd take the whole family. He'd buy the boy a basketball for his birthday. He'd— "Wait a minute!" his friends said. "Don't be so anxious to make him happy. Maybe his parents will think you're rich and sue you for hitting him. Maybe they'll claim he was injured!" In other words, maybe the family was corrupt, the way too many people are.

It was a warning Barry had to consider. He didn't really know the family. His lawyer advised him not to contact them for any reason. "You know how people are," he said. But Barry remembered the look of fear on the boy's face as the car struck him. "I didn't want him to grow up thinking that someone could hurt him and not care," he said. "It was worth risking some trouble." So he bought some baseball tickets— and he saw a little boy smile. "Maybe, just maybe, that boy will grow up knowing that everyone isn't out to get him," Barry said. That's something Barry certainly knows.

Gimme, Gimme!

I like to think I was ambitious when I started out in my career. But I'm afraid I was more than that—I was greedy. I wanted money, position and influence, and most people said that the way to get them was to be a good team player. It also made sense, they told me, to have a mentor, someone who could not only advise me but set a good example for me to follow.

Looking back now, I can see that my plans were doomed from the beginning. To begin with, I wasn't cut out to be a team player. And then I chose a mentor who never heard of the word *greed*. But he knew what *sacrifice* meant.

Frank was my boss when I went to work in a publishing house where I was to spend several years climbing up the editorial ladder. I knew very little about my work when I started, but Frank thought I had potential. He had much more important things to do, but he took the time to teach me everything I needed to know. He was demanding, but generous with praise. And when he discovered that I wanted to write, he stuck his neck out to give me opportunities to prove what I could do.

Frank didn't say much about himself, but I learned something about his history from other people. Apparently he had the potential for a brilliant career: he was intelligent, charming, sensitive, tough-minded and well educated. He had brought several publishers out of the red and into the black by finding the right authors at the right time. But he would not go along with the crowd. He lived by what he believed, and he said what he thought. His talents could have taken him right to the top of any organization, but his sense of justice and fair play kept getting him in trouble with higher-ups. I mean, you can't tell the publisher of a magazine that he ought to publish something worth reading instead of something that isn't worth the paper it's printed on. Yes, Frank was blunt. Consequently he had gone from job to job, although he was such a great editor that he always found another one.

When I met him, he was said to have mellowed, and he tried very hard to hold his tongue. He'd walk out of an editorial meeting and close himself up in his office—a warm, well-lighted, large room lined with bookshelves, with comfortable chairs facing a heavy old mahogany desk. He had the best office in the building, with windows on two sides, but he gave it atmosphere.

I had a chance to see Frank in action several times when he couldn't hold his tongue. He never spoke angrily; he spoke with passion. It broke his heart to see good books rejected and inferior work fussed over. He was also concerned about employees who had worked a long time for the company, and he kept pleading for a more generous retirement program. Frank couldn't get along with anything he thought wasn't fair.

One day he went too far. Objecting when a truly beautiful manuscript was pushed aside because its author wasn't well known, Frank banged his fist on the conference table and stood up. His dark eyebrows scowled fiercely over his light blue eyes, and his voice shook. "What are you in business for?" he said. "Do you *know?*" Then he left and went to his office.

The next morning, when Frank came to work, his office

was empty and carpenters were partitioning off part of it. He was shown to another office down the hall where his grand old desk took up almost all the space. New bookshelves would be built for him, he was told. The company was taking on more people and had to make room for them.

Frank never set foot in that new office. He worked at home and came in for meetings. Sometimes he would come into my office and we would talk about good books and the people we loved. They were precious moments for me—in the company of a man who really didn't care about money, position, or influence. He could have had them, and he knew it. But he never regretted the sacrifices he made. He was his own man.

Now, when I fight the good fight and wonder if it is worth the effort, I remember Frank. And I understand that even if I lose the fight, I haven't lost what God gave me to put into this world. That's important—because we're not here to get, but to give.

I—I—I

On one corner of my desk is a pile of papers I try not to see. They are letters I *really* want to answer. Some are more than a month old, but I don't have time to get to them. I'm too busy.

The truth is that I begin my day working on whatever is important to me and that's as far as I get. No doubt about it: I'm self-centered. Since I love to get letters, I realize that some people might like to get one from me. But it's easy to forget about other people when you're thinking about yourself. Especially when you have problems. And who doesn't?

Then why can't I forget about those letters? Because an aide in a nursing home taught me that I shouldn't.

Her name tag read "Roseann." She was a licensed practical nurse in a nursing home where a friend and I had gone to visit an elderly neighbor. She appeared to be in her early sixties; a short, stocky, vigorous woman with a round face that smiled as if she meant it. I noticed her because as soon as she appeared at the far end of the long corridor where many of the patients were sitting in small groups, heads went up. Something special was happening. All the way down the corridor, as Roseann stopped by each woman to say a few words or to pass out medication and see that it was taken—making a funny face to go along with it—a change took place. There were smiles, color came to pale cheeks, backs were straighter, eyes brightened.

When she came to our neighbor, she said, "Oh, Dora, I really like that sweater! Pink is your color, isn't it!" Dora pretended to be embarrassed, but she enjoyed the attention. "Roseann makes all of us feel good," she said after Roseann had left. "She spends time with us."

Several weeks later, when I visited Dora again, I looked forward to seeing Roseann. "Not today," Dora said, "maybe not ever." Roseann's husband had been killed in an automobile accident. Roseann had been with him and had done all she could to save him before the paramedics arrived. But nothing helped.

No wonder the corridor was so quiet. Not a head was up. Needlework lay untouched. There was no conversation—only a silent nodding, a meeting of eyes, and a turning away.

Visiting hours were almost over when the door at the end of the corridor opened and Roseann came in. She moved a little more slowly, but the smile was there, as generous as ever. And as she moved from one woman to the next, the room was filled with soft voices speaking words of care.

"I've got a treat for you," Roseann said as she approached Dora. In one hand she held a pill and with the other she offered Dora applesauce and a spoon in a paper cup. "Best chaser in the world," she said, screwing up her face as Dora obediently swallowed the pill.

Then Dora reached for Roseann's hand. "Thank you for coming back," she said. "We didn't expect you to—"

"I know," Roseann said, pressing Dora's hand. "I didn't expect to, either. But I kept thinking of how sad you all get around this time of day—and how much I like making you smile. I guess I need you, too. That's why I'm here."

I went home and began working on my letters. Not because it was the thing to do—but because I realized that I *need* to spend time in other people's lives. I feel at home there.

Chapter 6

❧

A Show of Strength

IT MAY NEVER HAPPEN to you. But it could. You may have to defend your right to be the person you are. And you may have to do battle with people you would rather befriend.

It happened to two of the gentlest, kindest people I know. Bill and Lucy had worked hard and saved hard for years to buy a small farm, which they got at a good price. It was within commuting distance of the city where Bill worked as a printer. Lucy got a job as a substitute teacher nearby. She also opened a small boarding kennel in one of the outbuildings on their property. She loved animals and remembered how hard it was to find dependable care for their own dog when they had to go away.

They spent every spare hour learning how to bring healthy crops out of the earth. It was something they had dreamed of doing. After a few years their farm was the kind that made you slow down and enjoy the view as you drove past.

Then one day when I called to make arrangements to

board my dog, Lucy said the kennel was closed. Temporarily.

"Why?" I asked.

A cluster of houses had been built on the fringes of the farm and the developer did not want a kennel for a neighbor. The developer did, however, want the farm, and he offered Lucy and Bill an extravagant price for the land. They refused to sell. The next day they received word that legal steps were being taken to close the kennel.

"Sell!" some of their friends advised.

"Forget about the kennel," Lucy's sister said. "Anything to keep the peace."

Bill and Lucy didn't agree. They consulted a lawyer who told them that a legal battle would be very expensive. A lot of legwork would be involved.

"Could we possibly do some of that legwork for you?" Bill asked. The lawyer said they could, but it would take an enormous amount of time.

Somehow they managed to do it. Getting up extra early, working through lunch, staying up late, they contacted all their other neighbors, most of whom stated in writing that the kennel was in no way a nuisance. They verified that the property was zoned for a kennel. They checked through old newspapers and records to prove that a kennel had always been part of the farm and could not be eliminated. That last bit of historical information won the case for them.

When the judge handed down his decision, Lucy asked him if she could make a public statement. It was unusual, the judge said, but he gave her permission. That was when everybody found out what Bill and Lucy had gone through.

Lucy's voice shook, but she took her time. "I just want

to mention some of the things that went on—things that weren't considered relevant to the case," she began. Then she told the court about the endless telephone calls late at night, and the heavy breathing on the other end of the line. And the other calls, when Lucy was home alone, and there *was* someone on the other end, and the words were threatening. And the garbage dumped on their land. And the broken fences. And the weed killer that ruined the cornfield.

"I'm glad we won this case, Your Honor," Lucy said. "But we can't very well celebrate. Somewhere out there among our neighbors, somebody really doesn't like us. And we don't know why. That's an uncomfortable feeling."

You will not avoid hostility by following Christ. Nor will you always be welcome. The friendliness welling up inside you may be rebuffed. Your sincerity may be mistaken for—of all things—deceit. Be assured that your gentleness will, at times, be interpreted as weakness. And your strength, should you have to summon it, may be resented.

Opposition will not always take place in a court of law or over a boundary line. It will accost you where you thought it never could: in your home, in your loves, where you care deeply. You will need a special kind of strength in those times. And you will find it. But the question is: *How will you use your strength?*

Why Put Up a Fight?

Remember when you were in grade school and you stuck up for your friends? Remember taking sides, and getting a little worried because there were so many more kids on the other side? Remember when you stopped talking to someone because you had an argument? Or when you told your sister to stop borrowing your boots without asking first? Or when you stood up to your brother and got to sit in the front seat of the car?

And then, as you grew up, you stopped all that nonsense. You found better ways to settle a dispute. You learned how to compromise and how to give up. You discovered that if you didn't take sides, if you stayed in the middle, if you didn't stand up, and if you kept your opinions to yourself, your life was more peaceful. People liked being around you.

Good for you—if you made it this far without losing something valuable: your identity. Because sometimes you have to be willing to do battle with someone who wants to change the person God intended you to be.

I grew up living in an apartment, and because our neighbors were so close—not only on each side, but above and below us as well—I was taught to keep my voice down and to walk softly. I was so accustomed to it that I never considered it an inconvenience. But one day new neighbors moved into the apartment below ours, and that very night someone banged on their ceiling to protest the noise we were making as we cleared the dinner table. For the rest of the evening we tiptoed and whispered.

The next evening my parents had a visit from the woman who lived below. She said I awakened her from a nap when I came home from school and "stomped" around the apartment. She also didn't approve of the way I ran down the stairs and along the hallway of the building. No one had ever complained about me before, and I was ashamed. I knew how important it was to my mother to keep peace with our neighbors, and I felt like some kind of a menace.

I tried, from that moment on, to make no noise at all. I didn't even talk to myself and I took my shoes off as soon as I came home. But even in my socks I seemed to irritate the woman downstairs because she kept complaining. My parents stopped listening to the radio, and after dinner, when they sat reading in the living room, the sound of the pages as they turned them seemed suddenly quite loud. Then one night I sneezed and we heard that terrible banging on the ceiling below us.

"I'll be right back," my mother said and left the apartment. I could hear her high heels tapping down the flight of stairs to the floor below and then the sound of a door opening. Then there was silence. My stepfather and I could hear voices, angry ones, coming from below, but we couldn't make out what was being said. Then the sound of a door, my mother's quick steps and she was back. With a smile on her face. "Put your shoes on," she said to me and turned on the radio. "Now—how was your day?" She said to my stepfather as she made herself comfortable in her favorite chair. We were back to normal.

I never knew what was said downstairs that evening, but the confrontation ended the complaints. It also ended the tyranny that had turned us into a frightened, anxious family —and I don't think that is what God intends anyone to be.

Anger—Something to Rely On

For a long time I was uncomfortable with Christ's anger. I preferred to think of Him as placid and accepting, and I tried to be the same kind of person. It seemed saintly to think the best of people, no matter what they did, to excuse the hurt they inflicted, to say, "I'm okay," even when I wasn't.

I didn't like to remember Christ calling people a generation of vipers. I winced when I thought of Him pushing past a crowd of followers, telling them to leave Him alone. I couldn't believe He would destroy a tree or turn on a disciple with a bitter denunciation. I couldn't deal with His fury against the temple vendors. His anger frightened me—because my own anger frightened me.

I used to feel wrong being angry. I thought I was supposed to love people, or at the very least, to like them. And if I was angry, it meant I wasn't loving. And if *I* wasn't loving, people wouldn't love *me*. Now, can you see why anger was so threatening to me? It meant the end of everything.

But I was mistaken. Because anger is a valuable, reliable, honest response to life. It happens even among people who love each other. It's an alarm that goes off when something is happening that we don't like. Not *like* as in *enjoy,* but *like* as in *feel safe with.* Anger tells us that we have a problem, and we must do something about it.

One summer a few years ago I was leading a workshop at a writers conference that I always enjoyed. I hadn't been feeling well the week before the meeting, but I assumed I had a minor virus that would go away. It didn't, and I barely made it through the opening day of the workshop. My head ached and I had terrible pains in my chest, so I thought I had better see a doctor. I asked around and called an understanding doctor who agreed to see me at the end of the day.

He found nothing wrong with me, but he said I was very tense. "I'd say maybe you're angry," he said, almost as an aside.

"Angry? *Me?*" I protested. "I'm not angry!"

"You sure?" he said, with a gentle smile. "Something has you tied up in knots—anger can do that."

My laugh sounded shallow. "I can't imagine what I'd be angry about," I said.

"Think about it," he suggested. "It's okay to be angry—but it's not okay to hold it in."

I went back to my room and tried to lie down, but it was hard for me to breathe, so I sat up. I tried to read, but the headache and pains in my chest made it impossible. I had no choice but to take the doctor's advice and consider why I might be angry.

It didn't take long for me to find out. I sat in my chair all night going over some relationships that gave me good reason to be angry—but until then I didn't want to admit it. Two business associates had failed to do their part of a joint project, and I was trying to finish the work myself. A friend was trying to persuade me to make an investment I didn't think was wise. My landlady was reneging on her agreement to let me sublet my apartment so that I could move into my house. Some money I needed badly, and had worked very hard to earn, was late coming in. Yes, I was angry! And had been for a long time. Except that I didn't think it was right for me to feel that way—not if I wanted people to love me.

My headache was a little better. . . .

Encouraged by my improvement, I dared to ask myself whether these troubled relationships would end if I made some of my own demands on them. Suppose I insisted that my two associates live up to their agreement or forget the project entirely? Suppose I said No to throwing my savings out the window? Suppose I held my landlady to her promise? Suppose I got on the phone and demanded my money? The answer was that the relationships probably wouldn't stand up to my demands—because they weren't good relationships to begin with. They lasted only because I had been so agreeable.

I was breathing more easily. . . .

These people weren't loving me. They were pushing me around.

No more chest pains. . . .

I was tired the next morning, but I had a wonderful feeling of freedom that got me through the day. At dinner that evening I looked at the people around me with a new appreciation. I had learned something about making relationships. They don't just happen. And you don't enter into them because you want someone to love you. You enter a relationship because you know who the other person is, and you know who you are. And you realize that you can give something to each other. Occasionally, in that kind of relationship, you may still have reason to be angry. But the relationship can handle it.

There was no need for me to fear my anger. It was telling me that some of my relationships weren't good—because they didn't allow me to object to something that wasn't fair. I couldn't blame that on the other people involved, because my anger was also telling me that I had misrepresented myself to them. Sure, I want to be loved, but as the person I am instead of the person others want me to be, and I didn't make that clear. Fair enough?

The Deed and the Doer

I know that we are supposed to love people in spite of what they do, but I find that difficult. Surprisingly, it was my dog Kate who helped me to understand how to make the distinction between what a person is and what a person does.

Most people—and that used to include me—think that an attack-trained dog is a vicious animal. Not so. Kate is a lovable, big German Shepherd who adores people. She even adores other animals and has a gentle way with a baby bird that falls out of a tree right in front of her. But she is trained to protect me. No, she will not chew you to pieces if you show up at my door. And, no, she will not attack you if you raise your voice, gesture extravagantly or have an argument with me. If you really want to harm me, that's another matter, and she can tell the difference.

Her protection training was a demanding experience for both of us. It began when she was a year-and-a-half old, almost fully grown, and accustomed to meeting people socially. In our first lesson Kate and I stood looking at the landscape when suddenly the trainer's "agitator," a man Kate had never seen, leaped out of the bushes and rushed at us as if he were going to attack us. Kate's response was very good; she didn't run. She stood her ground, placing herself between the man and me, and bared her teeth, lunging at him with all her strength. At the other end of the lead I had all I could do to stay on my feet, and even though I knew the man was pretending, he was so convincing that I felt the chill of fear.

The lessons got more complicated—because life is more complicated. "You don't want a dog who takes off after anybody who looks threatening," our trainer said. "Now she has to learn to discriminate between a hostile person and a hostile act." It took a long time, but finally Kate was able to sit by my side while the agitator walked past us in a suspicious manner, and even when he came right up to us and shouted some pretty terrible things. Kate kept her eye on him, but only if he raised his arm to strike us, or tried to kick us, did she seize him.

Then came the hardest part of all. Kate had to go for a walk with the agitator after one of our lessons. That meant she had to approach him in a normal manner, let him pet her and speak to her, and trust him to take her lead and walk off with her. I could sympathize with her apprehension as I led her up to the man, speaking in a pleasant voice. All she knew of him was the way he had behaved, and that was threatening. Nevertheless, she took her cue from me, although her ears were back and her body was tense. Then he spoke her name and offered her his hand, which she sniffed carefully. He went on speaking gently as he scratched under her chin, and gradually her ears came up. When she leaned into his hand, enjoying the massage, he took the lead from me and began to walk her in a large circle. Actually he was fond of Kate and regretted playing the "bad guy" in her life. He was also a very nice man, and I think Kate began to realize that. I won't say he became her favorite person, but eventually she liked him.

"Will she still go after him if he attacks us?" I asked the trainer.

"Wait and see," he said with an amused smile.

The next time the agitator came after us, Kate seized him as quickly as ever. But after the lesson, when he behaved respectably to her, she responded in kind.

I learned a lot from Kate's perceptiveness. I know now that I have to confront bad behavior, no matter whose it is. But I don't have to give up on the person.

Taking the Heat

I don't ordinarily think of Christ as a troublemaker. Nevertheless, to some people He was. He didn't have the usual credentials to speak in the synagogue, yet He spoke with authority. He claimed no title, yet He was a leader. He had no medical degree, yet He healed—mind, body and soul. Wherever He went, there were those who grumbled that He didn't know His place.

We all know what "peer pressure" means—that our friends like us as long as we do what they do. Usually we associate the term with teenagers. But don't kid yourself. Your peers can pressure you at any age to conform to what they think you ought to be.

Claudia is an excellent teacher who got a late start in her career. She went to college, got married, had children and then went back to school for her Ph.D. She had no difficulty getting a teaching position in a well-accredited university, but that was as far as she went. There were no promotions, no recognition, and always the threat that she wouldn't be granted tenure when the time came. To a teacher, tenure means that she is doing a good job, that the faculty knows it, and that she has a permanent position. In other words, she can settle down and concentrate on the business of opening young minds. Without tenure, she's like a paper cup that can be thrown away after it has served its purpose.

How does one get tenure? By earning the approval of people in authority. For some teachers, it's a snap. For others, it's a struggle. For Claudia, it was a battle royal.

Claudia didn't like to do research. And it was customary, in her university, for teachers applying for tenure to spend a lot of time doing research. Claudia did her research in the minds of her students. She prepared exhaustively for each one of her classes, but if a student didn't seem to understand the point she was trying to make, she felt it was her responsibility to explain her point more clearly. She was popular with her students, even with those who thought she asked a lot of them in return. She was the kind of teacher students came back to see years after they graduated.

When it was time for Claudia to apply for tenure, she was told that she didn't have a chance. She hadn't spent enough time on research in her subject. Of course, she could have thrown herself into a flurry of research and satisfied her critics, but that would have meant she had to cut down on the time she spent with her students—and that's where her talents were.

Claudia was not an aggressive person, but for the first time in her life she decided to fight for what she wanted. Who were these people who wanted to deny her a place on the faculty? Was everyone against her? Or were there some who thought she deserved to be among them?

Ordinarily, Claudia did not take people into her confidence, but this was an exception. She began to talk to her colleagues about her tenure situation, and she found that several of them were on her side. They thought she was doing a good job and was an asset to the university. They agreed to support her.

It didn't take long for word to get around that battle lines were forming. And that's when Claudia began to doubt herself. "A lot of people who used to like me don't like me anymore," she told me. "That's hard to take." She began to wonder whether she was becoming obnoxious.

Finally Claudia had to consider whether she herself liked what she was doing. And the answer was Yes. She was a good teacher trying to hold onto her place in the world, and that's something she would have applauded in anyone else. If some people were offended by what she did, they would have been offended by anyone else who did it. She could stop taking their opposition personally.

Claudia kept fighting until she got tenure. Along the way she found some friends she didn't know she had, and she lost some she had counted on. But the most important thing she gained was her friendship for herself. It kept her going when the heat was on.

When It's All Over

Confrontations are never easy for me, but I find it especially hard to confront people I love. I'm afraid I'll lose them. I'm afraid that if I insist on being myself when they want me to change, we won't be able to love each other.

Yet I wonder—does a confrontation always mean the end of love? Or can it strengthen the relationship?

One of my favorite families used to live next door to me some years ago. Then I moved and we didn't see each other for a long time. When we met again, we were very different people. We all were affected by the changes that happen so quickly in our world.

The Bensons used to be like the family on a Christmas card: Herb was the serious father, Nan the sensitive mother, and Cindy and Mark the adorable children. Herb looked after his insurance business, Nan looked after their home, and the children were looked after very well. They seemed to be happy and comfortable with each other.

The first thing I noticed when I saw them again was the tension in the family. Herb's business had done well, but insurance was a far more complicated field than it used to be. He had to spend much more time finding ways to keep his clients' premiums from rising. Nan had gone into real estate when the children grew up. She enjoyed her work, but the hours were unpredictable. Since so many people were working, most of them wanted to look at houses on weekends or at night.

Cindy was married and had a four-year-old daughter. But, as Cindy said, it takes two incomes to make it these days and she was looking for a job. Mark was in medical school and living at home—when he was home.

The tension came from the demands these four lovable people made on each other. Herb didn't like coming home to an empty house after a long day at the office. He didn't like making plans for the weekend and canceling them because Nan had to show a house. Nan tried to explain to Herb that she didn't have time to look after the house by herself; she was a working woman now. She kept asking Herb to run the vacuum around, and she tried to interest him in cooking, but he always found something else to do. She also wished that he would stop telling her how to be a real estate agent—as if she weren't capable of finding that out for herself.

Nan thought Cindy certainly would understand how she felt. But she was wrong. Cindy still thought of Nan as the mother who would make everything right. Would Nan look after her daughter when Cindy got a job? Why not? Nan was home, wasn't she? She didn't have to go in to an office every day, the way Cindy would.

Mark spent so many hours at school that he was rarely home. But Nan and Herb always knew when he was—from the food left out on the kitchen table, the plates that were never put in the dishwasher, and the laundry that accumulated in his room but was never put in the washing machine.

I missed the easy laughter when I was with the Bensons. I was uncomfortable with their sharp words to each other. They couldn't stay more than five minutes in the same room without getting into an argument about who didn't do what.

It was about a year later when I saw the Bensons again, and I was amazed that they were still together. Even more amazing was that they appeared to be happy—but in ways that were different from the Christmas card family I remembered. Herb had become an enthusiastic cook, and sometimes, when Nan had to show a house early in the evening, she came home to a home-cooked meal. When she talked about her work, Herb didn't interrupt to tell her how to close a deal, but he did say that Nan had been awarded a prize for the amount of business she conducted that year: they were going on a cruise. Housework was still a problem for both of them, but it was eased somewhat when Cindy, her husband, and daughter moved in with them. Now there were more people to pitch in. Even Mark does his own laundry. Cindy's daughter goes to nursery school when Nan isn't there to look after her.

"How did all this happen?" I asked Nan.

"It almost didn't," she said. "Herb and I almost called it quits, but first we decided to see a marriage counselor. And *he* called in Cindy and Mark for a family session."

"Wonderful!" I said.

"No, it wasn't," Nan said. "It was terrible! The counselor told us to describe exactly how we felt about each other and ourselves. So we started out being really polite and considerate—and then we started screaming at each other. We couldn't believe how angry we all were! But, you know, something very good came out of it. We all had the same problem—we were treating each other as if we were the same people we used to be. And we weren't! Nobody is. But we were trying to make each other go back in time and be the Mama, the Papa, and the Two Little Bears. Life doesn't let you do that—that's what the counselor told us, and we thought he was right."

I'm not surprised that Christ didn't hesitate to confront someone He loved. He knew that when we don't bring our differences out into the open, they can do more damage than confrontation can.

Chapter 7

&

So Much to Live For

I AM REACHING THAT age when I am beginning to wonder what will happen to me when I can no longer do some of the things I do now. Almost every morning I am out in the woods with my dog Kate, relishing the steep trails that take us high up into the hills. Someday I will have to give that up. Now, when I travel, I have the choice of going by train, plane or car. Someday that choice will be narrowed; someday I will need another person to take me where I need to go. One of my great pleasures in life is to make dinner for a few friends and enjoy some hours of good conversation; I won't always have enough energy. Today I think nothing of carrying bags of groceries into my house; someday the bags will be too heavy.

I value my independence. I make my own decisions, and accept the consequences; I live by my own schedule—where I choose and as I choose. How can I ever give that up? How can I ever submit to my own inability to carry out my wishes? To meet my own needs? How can I ever turn my life over—to someone else?

Yet that is what aging and death are all about: turning our lives over—completely—to God.

I thought, at one point, that I had given my life to Christ. Actually, I allowed Him to share it, because that's what I thought giving meant: the two of us sharing my human experience. Now I am beginning to realize that giving Christ my life means that I must eventually let go of my human experience and dare to begin a spiritual existence. I must eventually leave this world that has become so familiar to me—and go on to a world that neither I nor anyone else I know has ever seen. A world I only *believe* exists. I am talking about death. For some of us this transition comes suddenly, unexpectedly. For most of us the change occurs slowly, gradually: we get older.

I can believe that I am going to live forever, but I know that my life will not always be the same as it is now. And I am afraid of what I don't know. I cling—and will cling even harder—to what is familiar: to strength and unlined skin, to swiftness of step and clear vision, to plans and dreams and possibilities, to shoveling snow in the cold of winter and the splash of cool water in the heat of summer. From my vantage point, aging means that I must loosen my grasp on this life.

But when does a new life begin? And what am I to do in the meantime? I cannot believe that God means me to lie fallow like a wornout field.

Or does He?

If you have ever walked through fallow fields, then you know they are filled with life. Instead of crops sprouting from seeds recently planted, small animals and birds scout through the cut-down stalks and leaves, feeding on kernels, grasses, and husks that escaped the harvest. As you walk along, you might be surprised by the sudden uprushing of a bright-colored male pheasant who tries to attract your attention from the female in her nesting place among clusters of stems gone yellow and dry. A little later in the season a new generation will find shelter and warmth there.

Aging is a time of giving back out of what we have received. It is a time when God enables us to put something of ourselves into the lives of others. But it is also a meeting ground between the world we know and the world of God.

There is still much living to be done there.

Giving Something Back

The first time I met Helen Steiner Rice, she was in her late sixties and I was in my early thirties. It was the beginning of an extraordinary friendship.

I even remember what I wore: a navy blue suit with a pleated skirt and a frilly white blouse. And the reason I remember it is that Helen realized exactly what kind of an image I was trying to create and teased me about it forever after. I wanted to look businesslike—but not too much. It was the time when women were just beginning to assert themselves and we didn't want to come on too strong.

I needn't have bothered. Helen had been in business long before its doors swung open to women. She got there on talent and determination; image had nothing to do with it.

I was nervous meeting her. I was assigned to edit a book of her verses, and I wanted her to have confidence in me. She was very well known and I was afraid she might think I didn't have enough experience to work with her.

Helen lived in a hotel in Cincinnati. Her suite was furnished with her own possessions, which were as distinctive as her ornate signature: satin everywhere, on the chairs, sofas and chaises, the draperies and the braided ropes that tied them back in graceful swirls. The colors were pale—pink and green, mostly—and the carpet was thick and gentle underfoot. On the walls there were clusters of small paintings and photographs, gilt-framed, and everywhere you looked there were mementoes of her life—nothing that spoke of what she had done but many that told you what people meant to her.

Helen was a fancy dresser. I don't think she ever wore a suit, and her hats were famous not only for their height but for the yards of tulle and ribbons that adorned them. She was short, under five feet, and plump, with an oval-shaped face, serious eyes, and a high forehead. I'm saving the best for last: her hair was bright red, abundant and pulled up into an explosive rolled accumulation on top. She had very tiny hands and feet, and her hands moved incessantly. But, then, everything about Helen was in motion: her facial expressions, her thoughts and the words she chose to frame them.

She hadn't waited for me to arrive at her door; she came out in the corridor to meet me halfway. And as soon as we entered her suite she began to plan where we would go for dinner. Then we got down to business. She had a manuscript of her verses which she scrambled through rapidly as she recalled the reasons she had written each one of them. I tried to keep them in order as she tossed them aside, but she was too quick for me. "Don't bother," she said, "you can put them together in whatever way you like."

That evening, as we satisfied Helen's preference for a

Chinese dinner, I asked her whether I might see some of her more recent poems.

"There aren't any," she said, rather emphatically.

I didn't know what to make of that remark.

"Sometimes I don't write anything," she explained, helping herself to another portion of sweet-and-sour shrimp. "I just wait."

"For what?" I asked.

"For the Lord to give me something to write about," she said, as if I really should have known that all along. But then those quick perceptive eyes saw that I was at a loss. Wiping her lips daintily with a napkin and reaching for her glass of water, she said—in the most matter-of-fact manner—"I can't write a word without Him, so there's no use wasting my time until He's ready to give me an idea."

Helen never spoke in hushed tones about her Lord. He was too much of a close personal friend for that kind of language. In fact, she spoke of Him so easily that it made you wish you knew Him as well as she did. It also took you by surprise, because here was this worldly, successful woman with bright red hair and towering tulle hats who wasn't about to write another word unless God wanted her to.

I came up against that will of hers a few months later when I asked her if she had ever written any verses for fathers. The theme of the book of her verses was a celebration of the holidays, and she hadn't included anything that fit into Father's Day.

"Helen," I said gently but firmly, "this is a compilation of all our holidays. We can't leave one of them out."

"Well, I just never wrote anything that fits," she said,

and I could sense that she was getting ready to hang up. Obviously she wanted to get back to something else that was claiming her attention.

I knew I was taking a risk, but I had no choice. "Well, do you think maybe you could write one?" I said. But my voice wavered.

Silence.

More silence.

"Of course not!" she said and hung up.

I didn't know what to do. The theme of the book wouldn't work if she didn't have that Father's Day poem. Yet it seemed a shame to forego the book for that reason. I didn't know what to tell my company. Any way they looked at it, it was my fault.

The next morning I had a call from Helen. Very crisp and businesslike. "I'm sending you a Father's Day poem," she said, and I didn't dare interrupt her to say "Thank you."

"You're right, I *have* overlooked fathers," she went on. "And last night I had the feeling that God wanted me to say something to them. I don't know how good it is because it came to me very quickly. You'll have to judge for yourself." She hung up before I could say a word.

It was a beautiful poem. One of her best.

After that I felt that Helen and I had a good working relationship, so when I sent her the galleys of the book, I didn't anticipate any problems. But a few days later she called me, and it was a Helen I didn't know. Very brusque. Efficient. In command.

"This is not the way to put my poems together," she said, and I could picture her putting on her glasses. "You can't simply put them into categories like Christmas, Easter,

Labor Day and so on. You have to link one poem to another so that the reader gets an underlying message from the way they are arranged."

She paused and I knew she was giving me a chance to say something, but I was stunned. I had worked so hard on that book.

"Now," she said, "I'm rearranging the poems and I'll send them on to you in a few days. You'll see what I'm getting at."

When the cut-up and rearranged galleys arrived I spread them out on my desk immediately. And from the beginning I could see that Helen knew what she was talking about. She had made only small changes, but important ones. The way she put her poems together made the reader eager to go on to the next one. She was not only improving on my work but she was teaching me that the structure of a book was as important as the content.

The next day I called her and thanked her. At first she seemed to be in a hurry, but as I described what I had learned from her, she slowed down. "You really did a good job," she said, "but you have to remember something: you can't do anything well unless you feel strongly about it. And if you don't feel strongly about it, then you shouldn't do it."

"But I *did* feel strongly about your book," I said.

She was surprisingly gentle. "No," she said, "you felt strongly about *editing* my book. But you didn't feel strongly about each and every *poem* in the book."

Since that time I have never worked on anything I didn't feel strongly about. That was the first of many wonderful things that I learned from Helen. And I hope that someday I can pass them on to someone younger, as she did to me.

Something of Ourselves

I hope that when I am older I can leave a little something of myself in the lives of others. Not as a memorial to me, but as my gift to them—because I know what that kind of a gift means in my own life.

I think my life is richer because a woman named Zoe gave me the gift of facing reality. And I still can't throw away a book because a man named Ezra gave me my first real book when I was too young to read; I remember how it felt in my hands as we went through the pages together. I suppose you could say that these people are gone now, but to me they aren't. They never will be.

It was Pat Moran who gave me an insight into animals that made it possible for me to love them in a way they can understand. I met him many years ago when I was looking for someone to help me handle two lovable, scoundrelly, inexhaustible young Welsh Terrier puppies I had bought because I couldn't resist them. I knew nothing about the breed, and very little about dogs in general except that I had always loved them.

Brandy and Ben were housebroken, but that was all. They chewed everything in sight, they ignored me when I called them, and when I took them out for a walk, it was a circus. They kept getting tangled up in their leads, and that was always an excuse to wrestle with each other.

After making several calls to trainers listed in the Yellow Pages and being turned down repeatedly because no one wanted to take on two terriers—"Terriers! They're impossible to train, especially when there're two!"—I got Pat. He didn't say No. He just listened to my almost tearful tale of woe and said he would take a look at my dogs. That began a long and fascinating association.

Pat had been around a long time. He had won awards all over the world and set records that to this day haven't been matched. But I heard that from other people, not from him. He talked about animals, mine in particular and all others in general. He explained to me that animals don't think the way we do, so if we want to communicate with them we have to use the kind of language they can understand.

"You mean *I* have to learn to speak *dog?*" I asked.

He nodded.

"But how do I do that?" I said.

"First of all, you can take those dumb sweaters off them," he said gruffly.

The "dumb" sweaters were two matching yellow sweaters—with monograms—that I had knitted by hand. I had made them, not because I wanted my animals to look cute, but because I loved them and wanted them to be warm. But Pat explained that the thick double-coat of a Welsh Terrier was enough to keep him warm, and the sweaters simply got in the way.

"You're trying to turn them into people, and they're not," he said. "You've got to learn how to appreciate an animal for what it is, and bring out the best in him. And you can't do that by trying to turn him into something God never meant him to be."

I began going to Pat's place every Saturday afternoon, supposedly to train my dogs, but actually to train myself. I was learning that I had to be consistent with Brandy and Ben. I had to correct them *every* time they disobeyed a command, no matter how many other things I might be doing. I had to give them a command in the same manner every time, and in the same words. "Come" meant come. "C'mon" or "Hey" or "Here" meant confusion. I had to praise them every time they obeyed, and not take it for granted. I had to spend time with them. I had to give them exercise regularly. I had to look after their health and their diet from their point of view, not from mine. "No leftovers or snacks," Pat said. "Animals don't have the kind of digestive system that can handle our kind of food."

Something very wonderful began to happen. My dogs were not only behaving themselves, but we were becoming close to each other. We understood each other's language and each other's needs—and in many ways this is a relationship human beings rarely achieve with one another.

One day when I arrived at Pat's place he came out of his kennel office followed by a large black puppy who stopped and turned back the moment he saw me.

"Who's that?" I asked.

"A newcomer," Pat said. "Just let him be."

"Why?"

"Somebody's been pretty mean to him and I'm trying to straighten him out," he said, crouching down to scratch Brandy and Ben behind the ears. "I know some people who want to take him, but right now he doesn't trust anybody."

I was furious that anyone could mistreat an animal, and I wanted to pick up the little fellow and smother him with love. But Pat said I shouldn't even talk to him. "Let him come to you," he explained. "That's the way an animal is—he has to be sure you're not going to hurt him. Your intentions don't mean a thing to him. He needs to have proof—and that takes time. He's been here for three days and just this morning he started following me around. Pretty soon he'll want me to touch him—but I won't until he does."

Within a month the dog was Pat's buddy and ready to go to a home where he would be appreciated.

Our love for animals was a bond between Pat and me. He knew much more than I did, but he realized that I wanted to learn and he was generous with his wisdom. When he retired and moved west to breed horses, I missed him.

Pat died a few years later, and I grieved for a very long time. Something valuable was gone from my life—yet something remained. I don't just love animals now. Thanks to Pat, I know at least a little more about their part of our world and how to welcome them into mine.

A Meeting Ground

Last year I received a basket of flowers as I was preparing to go on a trip. So I took them to a nursing home in a nearby town where I knew they would be enjoyed. On my way out, I couldn't help noticing the rooms I passed on each side of me. They were bright and clean, and some of them had more personal touches than others, but it suddenly occurred to me that each room was a person's entire home.

I was very glad to get back to my house, which isn't large, but it's more than one room. I looked around at my furniture, and there isn't a lot of that, either, but each piece has a history that fits into my own history. I wondered how I could ever give up all these things. Or any of them, for that matter. How could I confine my life to one room? Would there be any point in living?

I'm still attached to this world, but I have a new friend—another Helen—who is teaching me how to give it up when the time comes. Helen Rapp is ninety-four years old. She lives in one room of the infirmary of a stately nursing home, and she spends much of her time in the presence of God. You notice that immediately when you meet her. It's the brightness of her eyes in spite of arthritic pain, and the easy, comfortable way she talks about going to be with God.

In fact, she's a little put out because God didn't call her two years ago when she was recovering from a gallbladder operation. "That's when I was supposed to die, and I know it," she says. "Nobody expected me to live. I was *so* sick, and the pain was terrible. I was ready to go. I've had a good life, an interesting life, and I wasn't trying to hold onto it.

"One night I had a dream—I could see Christ on the cross, and I said to Him, 'Oh, Lord, I'm in such pain that only You can understand how it feels. Except that Yours was much worse than mine.'"

The next morning Helen's doctor asked her if she would like to see the chaplain, and she nodded her head, too weak to say Yes. "He was such a lovely man," she said. "He sat with me and prayed for a long time and finally I went to sleep. I thought for sure I was dying, and it was beautiful. But then I woke up! And I started to get better and the pain went away. People couldn't believe it, but there I was. I still don't know why God didn't take me, but I guess He had His reasons."

Frankly, I'm glad God had His reasons because Helen is giving so much to me. She's a great reader, and she remembers books that I never knew. She knows a lot, or even a little bit, about almost everything—world events, medical progress, gardening, music, art, plus the other residents and the staff. As a child she went to a one-room schoolhouse and taught in one when she became a teacher, so I have a sense of history when I listen to her. When she shows me her blue-and-white gingham sampler displaying all the stitchery her mother taught her by gaslight after the evening meal, I feel as if she is bequeathing me a culture that is in danger of disappearing.

But the most important legacy that Helen gives to me is the assurance that there is more to life than the world I know. She talks about the big old house where she used to live, even for several years after her husband died, but she refuses to go back and take a look at it. "That part of my life is over," she says without bitterness. "This is my home now." And her room, even with its hospital bed, is homey with the small keepsakes that she could carry with her.

"It was the same with my car," she explained. "I always was a good driver, and my eyesight was all right—but my reflexes weren't as fast. That happens when you get older, even though they keep sending you a new driver's license. So one day I decided that it wasn't a good idea for me to drive anymore, and I stopped." She was surprised to discover how many friends were eager to take her wherever she wanted to go.

It's no surprise to me. I look at this woman with awe at the amount of time she has lived and participated in this world. But she looks ahead. She sees a glimpse of a world that you and I have not yet seen—and she knows that it will be a good place to live.

Chapter 8

Grace Has a Gentle Touch

I DON'T BELIEVE THAT grace is an extravagant gesture from God. He bestows it often, in ordinary ways, upon the most ordinary of us.

I can think of many times when I have used strength that wasn't mine. I have, in some situations, gone on trying after I had exhausted all my determination. I have stood my ground when I really didn't want to. I have been comforted when no one was in sight. I have been rested, even after a sleepless night. Wounds that a physician couldn't see, much less treat, have been healed.

Sometimes my needs seem to be more than I can ask God to meet. Such as the time, shortly after my marriage ended, when I was suddenly caught up in a dispute over the terms of a business agreement I had made with a friend. I had hoped to settle the dispute amicably, but for the first time in my life I was faced with the possibility of a court case. Until then I had had only the simplest, most ordinary contact with attorneys, so when I was called upon to give a deposition, I was terrified. Even though I didn't know what a deposition was, it made me feel as if I had done something wrong.

I was not in fighting shape. Emotionally I was recuperating from the wounds of a divorce. Physically I was exhausted from moving to a new address, beginning life as a single person, and putting extra time into my work. Financially I was counting pennies, and didn't know how I could afford legal fees. I was also stung by the unexplained hostility of someone I had known as a friend.

The burdens were more than I could handle. And although I knew I could call on God for help, I didn't know how to begin. It seemed to me that God would have to turn the world upside down in order to solve my problems, and I couldn't expect Him to do that.

I did what I could. I learned that a deposition meant I was to give my version of the facts, under oath, in response to questions from my opponent's lawyer. My lawyer also would be present to advise me. At a later date, my lawyer would take my opponent's deposition. It was, basically, the recording of information for use in a trial—or for one side or the other to press for an out-of-court settlement.

Then why was I nervous? All I had to do was tell the truth.

Except that, like most people, I had seen too many courtroom scenes in movies and on TV. I envisioned my opponent's lawyer trying to make me say something that appeared to be untrue—by interrupting me in midsentence, by demanding that I answer either Yes or No, by scowling at me, or by claiming that everything I said was irrelevant. I even began to question my own knowledge of the facts. Did I remember them correctly? Had I forgotten something? Was I going to discover that I *had* done something wrong without realizing it? After all, why would anyone want to sue me? I *must* be wrong!

I got some help from a friend whose work often required her to be in court. "You're partly right," she told me. "There may be an attempt to intimidate you. Sometimes it happens. But you *can* do something about it. Take your time. Think about what you want to say. Don't explain how you feel now or how you felt then—just explain what happened. And remember—you have your own attorney there to look out for you. So you're not alone."

All right. That was one problem solved, and I felt better. Until the night before the deposition when I went to bed and couldn't sleep. I had to get up very early the next morning and drive a hundred miles to New York and be more clear-headed than I had ever been in my life. *And I couldn't sleep!* My hands as well as my teeth were clenched. I stared up into the darkness and knew I was defeated. I was tired of struggling every minute, every day, in every area of my life. I didn't know what was going to happen to me, and I was losing the ability to care.

It happened quietly, slowly. I didn't see anyone or hear anything. But I knew God was there. I felt His presence as distinctly as I felt—yet couldn't see—the walls, the furniture, my sleeping dog in the corner of the room, the gilt-framed mirror and the two old flower prints over the chest of drawers. And I understood what He was saying: "*I* care." Nothing more. It was enough.

My mind and my body began to relax, and I thought I would fall asleep. But I didn't. I lay awake all night, very much at ease. I was in the company of God.

I wasn't a ball of fire the next morning and I was anxious about the deposition, but I was clear-headed. I still felt God's presence. It was true that I had run out of the ability to care, but Someone Else cared. I knew that whatever happened, however well or poorly I answered the questions, my mixed-up life was important to God. On that day I didn't have to count on my own energy; I had His.

The deposition went fairly well. My voice shook in the beginning, but then I remembered my friend's advice and took my time. I stuck to the facts. My lawyer was pleased. We shook hands and I headed home.

Right in the middle of New York City, during the evening rush hour, my car began doing strange things. The dashboard lights flashed red and the engine whined. I happened to be on one of the few streets in New York where you can find a gas station and I saw one a few blocks away. I made it—just at closing time. But the mechanic was still there, and seeing my out-of-state plates, he decided he couldn't very well walk away and leave me. At least, not after my engine gave up, which it did at that very moment.

An hour later my car had a new generator belt and I was coming out of the Lincoln Tunnel on the Jersey side, heading back to Philadelphia. It was getting dark and I was hungry. I realized that I hadn't eaten all day, which is unusual for me. I decided to stop along the way for a snack. Soup—I wanted a bowl of soup. Badly. It's what I always want when I am getting over something. That's when I knew I was able to care again.

I'm not saying that God took care of all my problems, because that isn't what happened. He helped, but there were things that I had to do as well. The case went on for two years before it was settled, and it was costly in terms of time, money and friendship. Gradually my energy returned and I began to rebuild my life. Once again I liked waking up in the morning. But during that critical time when I couldn't look after myself, God did. No one else could have understood what I felt, or given me what I needed.

I have been cared for. What I didn't have—and needed—God gave out of His own supply. I have known grace. So have you. But we don't always know it when it happens.

I used to think that grace was for heroes and heroines, for the winners in the world. It isn't. Grace is for losers, too. Grace is God getting as close to us as only He can. It is God's commitment to us, expressed in unexpected reminders that He is with us. Not only always, but in everything. Even when we don't ask Him to be.

Grace is God's assurance that we are loved and cared for.

Please don't misunderstand. Grace does not mean that we will be enabled to do everything we attempt. We will not always be understood. We will, sometimes, go down in defeat, no matter how good the fight we fought. Grace is not a victory march. It is God ministering to what we feel as a result of what we do in this world.

When Words Won't Do

I would like to love the way God does, but I'm a bit heavy-handed. I want to fix people up—right away, *my* way.

Take Libby—I liked her immediately for several reasons. She was serious-minded, intelligent, and she had a good sense of humor. She was a devoted mother, but the kind who spoke about her grown children as if they were her friends. Her husband traveled a lot and, after many years of marriage, Libby still looked forward to his homecoming the way that some of us look forward to weekends. She had a full-time job, yet she found time for volunteer work. If you needed her for anything, she was there.

Libby's only problem, as far as I could see, was her shyness. She didn't avoid people, but when she spoke she had an annoying habit of covering her mouth with her hand so that it was hard to hear what she said.

I decided to help Libby conquer her shyness. I thought she needed to have more of a social life. So I invited her to my home whenever other friends were coming to dinner, and I talked her into joining me at some professional events I thought she might enjoy. She was very popular—but the hand still went to her mouth when she spoke, and she began finding excuses to get out of my invitations.

"What's with you, Libby?" I said to her one day, when she said she couldn't go to a book and author luncheon because she had to get new snow tires. "You can get tires any day of the week."

I reached over and pulled her hand away from her mouth. "What am I doing wrong?" I asked her. "Why don't you want to go anywhere with me?"

Tears came to Libby's eyes and she turned her head away. I let go of her hand and she immediately clasped it over her mouth so that it was very difficult for me to hear what she said. Or was it that what she said was so hard for me to believe?

Libby told me that she was a recovering alcoholic. She began to drink heavily years ago when her children went to school and her husband was away on business for weeks at a time. She was lonely and she thought a few drinks would help. She could handle it. It was a story we've all heard before, and Libby wasn't trying to be original. She had hit bottom and almost lost the family that meant everything to her. Then she got help and began to recover. Except that alcoholics don't recover—ever. If they try hard enough, they are in the *process* of recovering for the rest of their lives. One drink, and they may slip all the way back to the bottom. Starting over again is that much harder because they can't kid themselves anymore. They know they're vulnerable.

I felt a lump in my throat that kept me from saying anything. I could only imagine how painful it must have been for Libby to get through the socializing I thought was so good for her. Of course, she didn't have to drink, but drinks were there. People were relaxed and laughing, talking in the easy way people talk when they're off duty—but Libby was fighting a desperate battle. And no one knew it. Each time didn't get easier; it got harder. And there I was, pushing her to have a good time.

Well, finally, everything was out in the open and Libby and I should have been able to go on from there. But that isn't what happened. We tried to remain friends, but over the years we lost touch with each other. I think we both were too embarrassed. Except that Libby had no reason to be. She hadn't misrepresented herself to me. *I* had misrepresented her to myself. I loved what I saw in her—and she did have those qualities—but I didn't have the grace to see what else was there.

Grace doesn't have to be told what someone needs. Grace feels as if the need were its own.

A Surrendered Mind

Sometimes I think it's my mind that gets in the way of any grace I might have. I don't like loose ends. I'm too quick to come up with a solution the minute I see a problem. Or is it really that I want to get the problem out of my way because it makes me uncomfortable?

Recently I woke up one morning with a lot on my mind. I felt I had gone too far advising a friend how to deal with a difficult mother-in-law. I was concerned about my stepfather because he seemed reluctant to drive long distances. Was he ill and didn't want me to know? Would he be too proud to let me pick him up and bring him to my house for the visits he used to enjoy? I was also putting in a lot of time on a book I was trying to finish—but something in me wanted to tear up the manuscript and start all over.

So you can understand what was happening: I was a wreck! And the day had just begun.

I did something I don't often do, and undoubtedly should. I stopped what I was doing, turned off the news program, and prayed. Not in tears or with desperate pleading, but in whatever words came to my surrendered mind. I asked God to let me lean on Him because I needed to get in touch with His love for me.

And then I tried to put my needs into words. I asked God to show me how to appreciate my troubled friend as she is, and to give her space to be herself, just as I must be given space to be myself. She needed my understanding, not my advice.

Then, as I began to see my problems more clearly, I *thanked* God for impressing my stepfather with the dangers of driving long distances at his age. And I asked for help in persuading him to let me come and get him—to tell him, quite simply, how much his visits meant to me.

I had been praying for the grace to give God's love to others. But I didn't realize that before I could give grace, I had to receive it, because grace is something we cannot imitate. We can only pass it on from God Himself to someone else. It was then that I felt God's love completely surrounding me. Warming and holding me close. And the pieces of my being began to come together. I could allow a friend's problem to go unsolved until that friend found her own way of dealing with it. I could live with the loose ends of my stepfather's struggle with his advancing years. Yes, I would be uncomfortable, because I would worry about these people I loved. But what they needed was for me to share their struggles—instead of shooing them away with a quick solution—just as God shares mine.

I think I am beginning to understand what grace is all about. It is God putting me to good use in the lives of my friends: sharing their sorrows, listening to their spoken thoughts and hearing what they cannot put into words, appreciating their joys—at a time when I have no power of my own.

A Full Life

Life is God's invitation to come and be of use in the world, but we don't have to accept it. We don't have to get involved. We can huddle in life's corners. We don't have to rock boats, make waves or cause ripples. We can stay here rather than head for there. We can bear up under rather than dig down into. We can use as little of ourselves as possible, and then wonder why life is so empty. Because, in spite of all we may possess or achieve, life becomes full only when we put more of ourselves into it.

Living boldly means using everything we've got—and that includes God. But if we do—if we grow spiritually—we have to be prepared to change.

Fine—for those of us who want such things. But not everyone wants to be bold. In fact, the word itself is not exactly attractive. It's almost—pushy.

It certainly is. It is Christ daring to enter a city where He isn't welcome. It is a woman, ordinarily reserved, elbowing through a crowd to receive the healing only He can give to her. It is a man risking dishonor, even death, to share with Him his struggle to believe. It is a child disobeying its elders to find appreciation in His arms. It is a frightened disciple coming out of hiding because he knows he is not the man he used to be; he is more. Knowing that we are cared about makes us pushy.

Why?

Because we have Someone to fall back on. Someone who can teach us how to look after ourselves. Someone who has work for us to do and knows we can do it. Someone who realizes that at times—perhaps often—we will fail, but Someone who knows that failure isn't the end of things. Someone who will help us get up again—if we need help, and we may not. Someone who doesn't mind starting over. Someone who will give us what we don't have—even if we don't want it—because it might come in handy. Someone who will lock arms with us against our fears. Someone who will take the pain we cannot bear. Someone who will understand our disappointments. Someone who will mend the parts of us that get broken, and not wince at our scars. Someone who finds us, pushiness and all, quite lovable. Someone who will prove to us—as He proved to others long ago—that He is with us. Always.

We are meant to live fully and boldly. We are meant to give and to get all the love we shall ever need. There is nothing—absolutely nothing—that can defeat us. There is no fear that can paralyze us. We are meant to share our experience with God, and to have—without even asking—the full power of His love in everything we do.

THE
PERFECT
COCKTAIL

THE PERFECT COCKTAIL

Hints, Tips, and Recipes from a Master Bartender

GREG DEMPSEY

MAIN STREET BOOKS

DOUBLEDAY New York London Toronto Sydney Auckland

A MAIN STREET BOOK
PUBLISHED BY DOUBLEDAY
a division of Bantam Doubleday Dell
Publishing Group, Inc.
1540 Broadway, New York, New York 10036

MAIN STREET BOOKS, DOUBLEDAY, and the
portrayal of a building with a tree are trademarks of
Doubleday, a division of Bantam Doubleday Dell
Publishing Group, Inc.

Book design by Gretchen Achilles
Illustrations © 1995 by Diana Jensen

Library of Congress Cataloging-in-Publication Data

Dempsey, Greg, 1969–
    The perfect cocktail : hints, tips, and recipes from a
master bartender / Greg Dempsey.
        p.   cm.
    "A Main Street book."
    1. Bartending—Handbooks, manuals, etc.   I. Title.
TX951.D42   1995
641.8'74—dc20   95-18953
                                                          CIP

ISBN 0-385-47914-X

10 9 8 7 6 5 4

CONTENTS

FOREWORD

The Perfect Cocktail does what no other guide to bartending accomplishes. Oddly enough, it explains how to bartend. Other guides do little more than simply list drinks. *The Perfect Cocktail* has put the focus where it should be: on the nuts and bolts of bartending. After all, a bartender, like a chef, must know more than just the recipes to succeed in his or her profession. *The Perfect Cocktail* explains every aspect of bartending from the most significant points to the smallest details; no aspect of bartending is left untouched.

Many other guides claim to be the official guides to bartending. For many reasons they are not. The Perfect Cocktail is an invaluable tool for the home bartender, the beginning bartender, and the established professional. It teaches the aspiring bartender the tricks of the old pro, yet is a great reference for the seasoned pro. *The Perfect Cocktail* was written by a bartender, not a writer, and for this reason it has all the information that is pertinent to the trade, without the fluff.

The problems with other bartending guides are many. Here are a few of the most common:

- Most other guides contain obsolete, and often incorrect, ingredients.

- Most other guides contain incorrect quantities.

- Many of the other guides contain far too many drink recipes, making them cumbersome reference tools.

- In most other guides, the important and demanding skill of making mixed shots is overlooked.

Let's look at a few of the differences between this guide and the other guides on the market. Many bartending books frequently have obsolete ingredients but *The Perfect Cocktail* includes modern ingredients. For example, most other guides have yet to replace recipes using lemon juice and powdered sugar with the modern-day equivalent found in every bar in the land, sour mix.

Incorrect quantities is another common problem with the other guides. Most other guides, including the self-proclaimed "official bartender's guide," Mr. Boston, has as its main ingredient for a Fuzzy Navel, 3 ounces of peach schnapps. In most bars throughout America, pouring 3 ounces of peach schnapps would constitute a double or a triple Fuzzy Navel, and would probably get anyone who poured that amount fired. A Fuzzy Navel does not call for 3 ounces of peach schnapps, in fact it does not call for any ounces, but rather a shot. A shot is an unregulated amount, usually somewhere between ¾ ounce to 1½ ounces, but each bar determines its own shot. The fact that the size of a shot is different for every bar is another important point which other guides fail to recognize. *The Perfect Cocktail* refers to all liquor (except wine) with respect to a "shot" not an ounce. After all, this is the language of the bartender.

Any bartender knows that although there are

thousands of drink recipes, there are only around fifty or sixty mixed drinks which are ever ordered. The other guides include hundreds, and in some cases thousands of useless drink recipes while lacking a section with just the most popular drinks. This guide includes plenty of fun drinks to make at home, as well as a comprehensive list of those most-ordered drinks. This chapter on America's most popular drinks will help the beginning bartender with easy reference to the bread and butter drinks. *The Perfect Cocktail* is designed to be a quick reference tool to be used behind the bar, not a large and clumsy dictionary of drinks that sits in the corner of the bar collecting dust.

It should be noted that there are many discrepancies with regard to drink recipes, especially those recipes for mixed shots. These discrepancies probably exist because other guides have neglected the importance of the shot. In fact, most do not even contain recipes for mixed shots. Discrepancies over drink recipes are most apparent between regions of the country. However, differences may also exist between bars and even between bartenders in the same bar. *The Perfect Cocktail* has made every attempt to use the most widely accepted recipes for each drink or shot. It is *The Perfect Cocktail*'s purpose to bridge this gap and become the undisputed authority on drink recipes.

Mixed shots are the most demanding part of modern-day bartending. So *The Perfect Cocktail* includes a section devoted to this facet of bartending, something which is absent in most other guides. *The Perfect Cocktail* gives you the ingredients for a great number of these shots and the instructions in the difficult and often nerve-racking task of making them. This guide has included over a hundred recipes for mixed shots because, unlike mixed drinks, patrons will often give a description of the type of shot he or she wishes to try and allow the bartender to use his or her discretion in choosing a shot to fit the description.

Finally, and as important as any of the points above, this guide gives the aspiring bartender the basic knowledge to succeed in this often-demanding profession. Unlike other guides in this field, *The Perfect Cocktail* gives the aspiring bartender shortcuts and tricks of the trade for behind-the-bar success. In short, *The Perfect Cocktail* makes bartending easy to learn.

BARTENDER'S RESPONSIBILITY

If misused, alcohol can be very dangerous. Drunken driving is the most serious problem relating to alcohol. It is by far the leading cause of automobile fatalities in the United States today, accounting for nearly half of all highway deaths. For this reason, bartenders should monitor the alcohol consumption of their customers and guests.

THE SIX GENERAL DRINK CATEGORIES

The Perfect Cocktail has created a classification system to better aid in explaining how to make mixed drinks. This new system classifies drinks into six general categories. The categories are not determined by how drinks are mixed, the basis of the old system, but rather on a combination of these factors: quantity of liquor added to the drink, number of liquors added and whether combined with mixer/s, and whether or not the drink is served with ice.

1. ONE-LIQUOR DRINKS

One-liquor drinks obviously have only one liquor and usually require just one shot of that liquor, unless otherwise requested (i.e., a double vodka and tonic).

EXAMPLES:

RUM AND COKE
- 1 shot rum
- Cola

Serve.

SCREWDRIVER
- 1 shot vodka
- Orange juice

Serve.

2. TWO-LIQUOR DRINKS

Two-liquor drinks require a combined total of between a shot and a shot and a half of two liquors. This combination is not necessarily equal parts of both liquors. For instance, a White Russian calls for more vodka than Kahlúa. When making a two-liquor drink on the rocks, it is important to have a full glass of ice because it will make the drink appear larger when in fact it is a small drink, though quite a lot of liquor. Because of the additional liquor, two-liquor drinks are more expensive than those drinks containing just a shot.

EXAMPLES:

MANHATTAN
- 1 shot American whiskey
- ½ shot sweet vermouth

Stir and garnish with a cherry.

WHITE RUSSIAN
- 1 shot vodka
- ½ shot coffee-flavored liqueur (Kahlúa)
- Cream

Shake.

3. MULTI-LIQUOR DRINKS

Multi-liquor drinks require a combined total of approximately two full shots of three or more liquors. These drinks can be difficult to make when you begin bartending, but with practice you should get the hang of pouring them. Remember: due to the greater amount of alcohol in multi-liquor drinks, these drinks will be more expensive than one- and two-liquor drinks.

EXAMPLES:

ALABAMA SLAMMER

- ³/₄ shot amaretto
- ³/₄ shot Southern Comfort
- Splash of sloe gin
- Orange juice
- Pineapple juice

Stir.

LONG ISLAND ICED TEA

- ½ shot vodka
- ½ shot gin
- ½ shot rum
- ½ shot tequila
- Splash of triple sec
- Sour mix
- Splash of cola

Garnish with a lemon slice and serve.

4. ON THE ROCKS

On-the-rocks drinks, often referred to as simply "rocks," require a small rocks glass filled with ice and a combined shot and a half of the desired liquor, liqueur, or denoted mixer. The term "on the rocks" not only means on ice, but more importantly a shot and a half of the combined ingredients. Because some people hear the term "on the rocks" and think it only means "on ice," you may have to enlighten them to the increased amount of liquor. When making an on-the-rocks drink it is important to *fill* the glass with ice. If the glass is not completely filled with ice a drink served on the rocks will look as if the bartender underpoured the drink. It will appear this way because an on-the-rocks drink has only a shot and a half of combined ingredients. This may be a lot of liquor, but it is not a lot of liquid, and will look very small even in a small rocks glass.

Note: Today, many of the drinks that originate as shots are being ordered on the rocks (i.e., Sex on the Beach, Russian Quaalude, etc.), and for this reason it is a good idea to ask patrons whether they would like the drink as a shot or on the rocks.

EXAMPLES:

SCOTCH
- ¹/₂ shots Scotch whisky
Serve.

RUSSIAN QUAALUDE
- ¹/₂ shot Stolichnaya (Russian vodka)
- ¹/₂ shot hazelnut liqueur (Frangelico)
- ¹/₂ shot amaretto
Serve.

5. STRAIGHT UP

Sometimes shortened to "up." This category of drinks calls for a shot and a half of the desired liquor or liqueur served without ice in either a brandy snifter or a cocktail/Martini glass. Drinks ordered "straight up" may or may not be chilled; those which are chilled are similar to on-the-rocks drinks but are served in a different glass and without ice. If chilling is required, do so in a shaker and strain into a cocktail glass. If requested unchilled (almost always either a brandy or a straight liqueur), pour straight into a brandy snifter.

EXAMPLES:

GRAND MARNIER

- 1¹/₂ shots Grand Marnier

MARTINI
REQUESTED "STRAIGHT UP"

- 1½ shots gin
- Splash of dry vermouth
- Desired garnish

Strain from shaker with ice into cocktail glass. Garnish.

6. SHOTS

Because shots are the most discretionary aspect of the bar business, the size of a shot will vary from bar to bar. Shots range anywhere from ¾ ounce to around 1½ ounces (rarely larger). The given bar's management will determine the size of the shot. This is why *The Perfect Cocktail* deals with all alcohol in terms of shots, not ounces. Straight shots require a total of one shot of a given liquor or liqueur. Mixed shots require different liquors, liqueurs, and mixers combined for a total of one shot.

EXAMPLES:

WHISKEY
(STRAIGHT OR NEAT SHOT)

- 1 shot whiskey

B-52 (MIXED SHOT)

- ⅓ shot coffee-flavored liqueur (Kahlúa)
- ⅓ shot Irish cream
- ⅓ shot Grand Marnier

Layer.

THE THREE WAYS TO MIX A DRINK

THE HIGHBALL

The mixing of a highball is done directly in the glass that will be served to customers. Today many drinks originally intended to be served in the highball or large rocks glass, including most drinks containing carbonated mixers, are generally served in the small rocks glass.* The highball is the easiest drink to mix: simply add the drink's ingredients into the glass and serve. There is a chronological process which should be followed in making any highball.

The first step in creating a drink is choosing the proper glass for the designated drink and filling it with ice. Unless ordered "straight up," all drinks are served with a full glass of ice. The full glass of ice is not only to keep the drink cold, but also to give the drink a stronger taste of alcohol. If the drink does not begin with a full glass of ice, the drink will require a greater amount of mixer to fill the glass, the alcohol will be too diluted, and it will therefore taste like a weaker drink. Weak-tasting drinks translate into unhappy customers and lower tips.

The second step is adding the different ingredients to the glass. As might be expected, this is the part of making a mixed drink which requires the

*This is probably because bars realized they could increase the number of drinks they serve and decrease the amount of mixers they go through by serving most highballs in the small rocks glass.

most skill. The addition of liquor should be very exact. To add the proper amount of liquor, use either a jigger or free pour (see section on "Free Pouring," page 17).

The addition of mixer is less exact. If there is only one mixer (like Coke in a Rum and Coke), it is added after the liquor and should fill the remainder of the glass. To avoid spillage, you should fill to about half an inch from the rim of the glass. If there are two primary mixers as in a Bay Breeze (orange juice and cranberry juice), equal parts of each are added. This guide does not place measurements next to most primary mixers. This is because primary mixers should fill the glass after the liquor has been poured. With two primary mixers, the first mixer fills the remainder of the glass halfway, the second mixer fills the glass to the top.

Examples of secondary mixers, such as Rose's lime juice, grenadine, or Tabasco, make up only a small part of a drink. In most cases, secondary mixers can be added either before or after primary mixers. Secondary mixers are usually strong-tasting, and therefore should be added sparingly. These measurements will usually be either a dash (less than a teaspoon) or a splash (a little less than ½ an ounce).

After the addition of the various mixers the drink is ready for the garnish. Depending on the garnish and if time permits, give it a squeeze and drop it into the drink. Complete the drink by adding a straw or mixing rod, and serve.

THE CHRONOLOGICAL ORDER IN THE MAKING OF A MIXED DRINK

1. Garnish the rim of the glass, usually with salt or sugar (this is only done on a handful of drinks).

2. Fill the designated glass with ice.

3. Pour the primary liquor into the glass.

4. Pour the secondary liquor into the glass.

5. Pour the primary mixers into the glass (in most cases steps 5 and 6 are interchangeable; however, certain drinks require step 6 to follow step 5).

6. Pour the secondary mixers into the glass.

7. Add the garnish to the glass.

8. Add a straw or mixing rod to the drink.

9. Serve with a coaster or napkin.

When more than one drink is ordered at the same time it will speed the process considerably if the bartender makes the drinks simultaneously. This is done by lining up the glasses as close to each other as possible, then adding ice to those glasses which require it. Drinks having common ingredients should be made next to each other. For example, if the drink order calls for two Vodka and Tonics, a Gin and Tonic, a Screwdriver, and a Bourbon on the Rocks, the bartender should line up four small rocks glasses followed by a large rocks glass, all to be filled with ice. The bartender begins by pouring a shot and a half of bourbon into the first rocks glass, the Bourbon on the Rocks is now complete. The bartender then pours a shot of gin into the next small rocks glass. He or she is now ready to proceed to the remaining drinks, which call for vodka. A shot of vodka should be poured into each of the remaining glasses, one into each of the small rocks glasses and one into the large rocks glass. It is now time for the mixers. First fill the three glasses in the middle, the Gin and Tonic and the two Vodka and Tonics, with tonic water. Now fill the large rocks glass with orange juice to complete the Screwdriver. Garnish the tonic drinks with lime wedges. Add mixing rods to the drinks served in the small rocks glasses and a straw to the Screwdriver served in the large rocks glass. Finally, serve the drinks. This method has no wasted time or tasks. Each bottle and mixer is pulled out and used only once. At first, mixing a number of drinks at the same time will be confusing, but with practice it will come naturally.

SHAKEN AND STIRRED DRINKS

In the past, the making of shaken and stirred drinks was a practice that was strictly adhered to. Today, though making a small comeback in certain areas, the practice has been all but abandoned by many bars and bartenders. Today, the only way to assure that a drink originally intended to be shaken or stirred will be mixed as such is if it is ordered "straight up, chilled." Of course, one can still order a drink "shaken" or "stirred."

There are several reasons for the move away from shaken and stirred drinks. The first reason for abandoning this practice is because of the public's shift from the straight-up cocktail to the on-the-rocks drink. Now most drinks originally intended to be served in a cocktail glass "straight up, chilled" are overwhelmingly ordered "on the rocks," most notably by the younger crowd. This change in tastes is probably because a drink over ice is not as strong as a drink straight up; the ice dilutes the mix, weakening the drink. Today's preference for on-the-rocks drinks means that it is not as important to shake or stir a drink, but it is a skill every bartender should know. The main reason for shaking or stirring a drink was in fact not for mixing, but rather for chilling. Because most drinks originally intended to be shaken or stirred are today served on the rocks, no outside chilling is needed. However, it is essential to know how to mix a straight up, chilled drink. The final reason that shaking and stirring drinks has been neglected is that in busier bars where time is short, pouring drinks as if each were a highball, needing no mixing, saves valuable time, thus allowing the bar and bartender to make more money. Though these mixing practices have declined in recent years, it is important to know how to perform each act. The drink recipes in this book denote the intended mixing technique for each drink.

THE SHAKEN DRINK

To shake a drink the same guidelines are used as for making a highball, except that the ice and ingredients are not added directly to the glass the drink is served in, but rather they are added to a mixing glass used in conjunction with a metal tumbler. Pour the mix into the mixing glass because it is smaller and will fit into the large metal tumbler, and mix. Unless mixing many drinks, I recommend that you not measure drinks in a tumbler because it may contain too much liquid for the serving glass to handle. After adding the ingredients into the mixing glass, secure the mouth of the tumbler over the mouth of the mixing glass firmly pressing it to form a water-tight seal. You just made a "shaker." Hold both components of the shaker together and shake it in an up-and-down motion, making sure the mix goes back and forth between both mixing glass and tumbler. Now place the shaker down, the tumbler facing up, and break the seal which has been created by hitting the tumbler with the butt of your hand. Remove the mixing glass and strain the contents of the tumbler into either a cocktail glass or a small rocks glass with or without ice.

Though most bartenders only shake drinks served straight up, you may be asked to shake a drink ordered "on the rocks." The most efficient way to do this is to use a short shaker. A short shaker allows you to shake the drink using the glass it will be served in, thereby eliminating the straining of the drink as well as excess glasses to be cleaned. Simply place the short shaker over the intended glass containing the mix, shake the drink, then simply remove the metal tumbler, garnish the drink, and serve. Don't forget to clean the shaker after using it.

The rule of thumb for knowing when to shake drinks is to do so when a drink has a large number of ingredients, because they will need shaking to properly mix. You should also shake drinks that have ingredients that don't easily mix, such as cream or sour mix.

THE STIRRED DRINK

A stirred drink can either be made in the glass it will be served in, if it will be served on the rocks, or added to a tumbler first if requested "straight up." If a drink is ordered "on the rocks" it is faster to stir it in the glass in which it will be served, and this will not create excess instruments to be cleaned. To make a stirred drink, simply add the required ingredients to the glass, stir the drink once or twice with the mixing rod, and serve. For stirred drinks which are ordered "straight up," combine the ingredients in the tumbler and stir the mix with either a long bar spoon or a long mixing rod. Some bartenders will swirl the tumbler in a circular motion to mix and chill the drink. Though this is not technically correct, it is faster, and to most drinkers the difference in style goes unnoticed. The drink is now ready to be strained from the tumbler into a cocktail glass, garnished, and served.

POURING LIQUOR

Possibly the most important part of bartending is pouring liquor. The bartender must pour the correct amount of liquor in each drink. An old bartender saying is, "Short neither the house nor the customer." In other words, pour the exact amount ordered.

USING A JIGGER

The beginning bartender should use a jigger until he or she is an accurate free pourer. The jigger will regulate the amount of liquor you pour. Because bars use different shot sizes, there are different sized jiggers depending upon the bar you work in. Each bar should have only those jiggers which will properly regulate its specification of a shot.

To keep customers happy, only fill the jigger about three quarters full before pouring the shot into the glass. Then while pouring the three-quarters full jigger into the glass, continue pouring the remaining quarter of the shot directly into the glass; this amount is so small you can eyeball it or use a count (see below). Doing this will give the customer the illusion that he or she is receiving a generous pour when in actuality only a shot is being dispensed.

In time, and if allowed by the "house" (the bar), a bartender will graduate from using the jigger and move up to free pouring. Free pouring will save the bartender valuable time, and it also looks more professional. To free pour accurately, one must be able to pour a given amount of liquor (i.e., shot, shot and a half, double) without using a jigger. To accomplish this a bartender uses a count. A count depends on two factors: the rate of flow of the speedpourer (this is a device which is placed over the mouth of the bottle and regulates the flow of liquid); how fast the bartender silently counts. The brand or model of the speedpourer must never change or the count will have to be altered to the rate of flow of the new pourer. It is also important that the bartender always hold the bottle at the same spot, the neck of the bottle, and when pouring hold the bottle completely upside down. Place all speedpourers facing away from the label of the bottle to which each is affixed, so that when pouring, customers can read the label. Then place each bottle in the speed rack with its speedpourer facing forward. The spout of the speedpourer is normally angled, so in order to get an even flow of liquor the speedpourer must face forward. The second factor is completely subjective. Count at whatever rate you desire, but you must be consistent. Your consistency will determine your precision at pouring exactly a shot every time. Most bartenders count in their head using numbers, which is what I recommend, yet anything can be used as a count, including letters, words, or whatever. *The Perfect Cocktail* recommends a four count for a shot. A four-count shot means each count is equal to a quarter shot. Using a four-count mode, a two count would be half a shot, a six count would be a shot and a half, and an eight count would be a double.

To determine your count, fill an empty liquor bottle with water and place a speedpourer over its mouth. Then practice your count while trying to pour a perfect shot into a jigger or shot glass. You will most likely have to adjust your count to coincide with the rate at which the shot is poured. Remember, a shot's size is dependent upon the bar in which it is poured, therefore use a jigger or shot glass which represents the size shot which your bar endorses. If there is no speed pourer, the flow of liquor will be unregulated, and you will have to measure liquor with a jigger or a shot glass. With practice, an aspiring bartender should be able to free pour efficiently in very little time. The beginning free pourer may have trouble keeping count the first few nights in which he or she is busy. If this is the case, simply revert to using the jigger until you feel comfortable free pouring in a pressure situation.

MIXED SHOTS, SPECIALTY SHOTS, SHOOTERS OR SHOTS

Mixed shots are a difficult and demanding part of bartending. Success in making shots will only come with practice. Shots that are layered or served unchilled are relatively easy to make because they are poured directly into the shot glass. The difficulty in making shots that are chilled in a shaker is in knowing the correct amount of ingredients to add to the mix, because there is no glass regulating the amount of mix to add. Because *The Perfect Cocktail* gives its shot ingredients in fractions of a shot, simply multiply the fraction by the number of shots to be made in order to arrive at the proper quantity. For example, if a group of people ordered five Alabama Slammer shots, each of the five ingredients in the mix calls for a fifth of a shot, therefore one shot of each of the five ingredients would be called for to complete the order. That was easy. Let's say there were seven shots ordered for the same shot, a more difficult calculation. In this instance we know that a total of seven shots will be needed. We also know that each of the five ingredients makes up one part of the shot, therefore we will need a little over 1¼ and a little under 1½ shots per ingredient. There is no time to get out your calculator; this is where your eye, your intuition, your bartending skill, and maybe even a little luck come in handy. Simply wing it. It is important to relax when making shots. They can be difficult to create, but take comfort in knowing that because they are consumed or "shot down" so fast and are so small (only around an ounce), it is very difficult to distinguish a problem with a shot unless you really screwed up the recipe. In time and with practice you will gain the ability to efficiently complete the requested shot order.

The majority of mixed shots call for chilling. When making chilled shots fill your shaker with ice followed by the shot's ingredients. After the mix has been shaken in the shaker it is ready to be poured. At this time, line up the correct number of shot glasses for the order in a tight row. Each shot glass should be touching the glass next to it (see illustration). If the glasses are touching each other, the pouring process will be more efficient, allowing you to continue pouring while going from one shot glass to the next. You are now ready to dispense the shots from the shaker.

If using a Boston shaker, which consists of a metal tumbler and a mixing glass, and if the shot order is small enough, dispense the shots from the mixing glass instead of the tumbler. Using the mixing glass will allow you to see the mix through the glass while pouring the shots. Place the strainer over the mouth of the mixing glass or the tumbler and begin pouring at one end of the row of shot glasses. Work toward the opposite end filling each glass approximately half full with the mix. When you reach the opposite end, fill the final glass ap-

proximately three quarters full and then work back toward the end which you began. This second pass should find each half-full shot glass being filled an additional quarter, so when this second pass is complete each shot glass will be approximately three quarters full. With each glass three quarters full, if you run out of mix at this time the glasses are sufficiently full to allow them to be served. However, if there is more mix in the shaker, make another pass or two until the shaker is empty or all of the shot glasses are full. Because estimating the correct amount of ingredients to add when making multiple shots is difficult, we recommend this technique to allow for some degree of error in the quantity of the mix. We do not suggest pouring one glass after another until each is filled. The problem with this method is that when you arrive at the last glass there may be no mix left or only enough to fill it part way. The drink order will be much more attractive and professional looking if each glass is equally full.

LAYERED DRINKS

Some drinks, most notably shots and pousse-cafés (multi-liqueur drinks, best served in a cordial glass), are designed to be layered. Layering is when a drink's ingredients are poured so that they are layered one on top of the other, like oil and water. This is done to make the drink taste and look better. Recipes for layered drinks are always given in the correct order for layering. The rule of thumb for layering is always to pour the heaviest liquor first followed by lighter and lightest liquors. However, just pouring the ingredients in correct order is not always enough to produce a successful drink. To help in the layering process the liquor is poured gently over the back side of a spoon, which slows and spreads the flow of the liquor, keeping it from mixing with the heavier liquors already in the glass. If there isn't a spoon handy or there isn't enough time, pour the liquors in a slow and careful manner.

Floating is a form of layering in which only the top liquor is layered, and is often done with mixed drinks. To float an ingredient on top of a drink (in a Harvey Wallbanger, Galliano is floated), simply pour the liquor slowly and carefully into the glass. It is best if you pour over ice already in the glass at the top of the drink. The ice will stop the downward flow of the liquor, keeping the given liquor from mixing with those ingredients already in the glass.

FLAMING ALCOHOL

Before you serve flaming alcohol make sure that the bar permits this practice. When flaming alcohol at home, make sure not to flame near curtains, draperies, paper, or anything else which is flammable. Depending on the proof of the liquor, you may have to warm the alcohol so that it will light. Liquors with proofs over 100 don't need to be warmed prior to flaming.

There are several basic safety rules you need to abide by when flaming drinks. Never flame alcohol in a bright room or in the daylight. Flames from alcohol are nearly invisible in a bright room, so you should only flame in a dark room where you can keep track of the flame in case there is a spill. Never use large amounts of alcohol to flame drinks. A good technique for flaming drinks is to warm a teaspoon of liquor, ignite it, then slowly pour the flaming liquor into the prepared drink. This is safer and easier than lighting the liquor right in the glass. Never pour liquor from a bottle into a flaming dish or drink, because the flame may travel up the stream and into the bottle. Keep flaming alcohol at arm's distance, as it may shoot up from the glass or dish at any time. I also advise avoiding flaming liquor on nights in which the bar is very busy; it is possible a patron could accidentally be pushed into the bar, spilling the flaming drink.

If someone requests a flamed drink, the safest are the Lemon Drop shot and the Cordless Screwdriver. Flaming either of these shots is optional and can be done by pouring a splash of 151-proof rum over the slice of lemon or orange. Ignite the slice which sits atop the shot glass and view the flame. The flame will be short-lived but will present little danger. To ensure safety, any other drink that is flamed should be extinguished prior to drinking. This can be done effectively by covering the top of the glass, eliminating the supply of oxygen. Place a damp napkin in the palm of your hand and quickly cover the top of the glass with it.

FROZEN DRINKS

Making frozen drinks is another part of bartending that is often difficult for the beginner. The reason is that frozen drinks are not made in the glass they are served in, but rather in a blender. A trick for new bartenders is to combine the ingredients directly in the glass in which the drink will be served, then pour the contents of the glass into the blender. Doing this will insure that the right amount of mix is added to the blender. After you have had some experience in making frozen drinks, you should be able to gauge how high the blender should be filled for one or more frozen drinks.

If a frozen drink order comes in along with several other drinks, make the frozen drink first. This will give you ample time to work on the rest of the order during the "dead" time while the drink is being blended.

To make a frozen drink, first add the shot of primary liquor followed by the secondary liquor (if called for). At this point add the mix or fruit. Next, add any secondary mixers. Finally, add approximately one cup of ice (8 ounces). This amount as well as the amount of mixers added will depend on the size of the glass in which the drink will be served. Remember, bar glasses come in all different sizes, so add ice to the blender accordingly. The mix is now ready for blending. If it is an especially thick mix, you may want to start the blender on low speed, and as the mixture becomes more viscous adjust it to high. The drink should be blended in fifteen to forty seconds, depending on several variables including room temperature, the temperature of the mix, the power and speed of the blender, and the sharpness of the blade. With time, you will be able to gauge all of the above variables. A rule of thumb for blending is that the drink is usually about done when the condensation on the outside of the blender reaches the height of the mix within the blender. After the drink is done blending, it should have about the same consistency (or just a bit thicker) than that of a convenience-store Slurpee. For a slushier drink, simply add more ice. The drink is now ready to be poured, garnished, and served.

Making multiple frozen drinks is very similar to making multiple chilled shots. In both, the beginning bartender may find it difficult to add the right amount of ingredients to the mix, especially when making a large order. Therefore, the pouring technique for making chilled shots should also be utilized when making multiple frozen drinks. If you haven't made enough mix for a three-drink order—something which can happen to even a veteran bartender—you will have a problem if you fill the first two glasses and only have enough to fill the third glass halfway. Being half a glass short and balancing it out over three glasses is fine.

GARNISHES

The first thing a bartender should do when he or she starts a shift is to make sure that there are enough garnishes, and if there are not, to cut enough to last the night. Garnishing a drink is the easiest part of making a drink. All you really need to know to properly garnish a drink is how to cut the garnishes. Cutting garnishes is part of the daily routine for a bartender. The garnishes which require cutting are limes, lemons, and oranges. All other garnishes are simply placed, as is, into the drink.

Limes:
These are cut in half and then into wedges (quarters or thirds of the original half cut). Squeeze the garnish over the drink then drop into the drink. If you have ample time, rub the lime around the rim of the glass, it will add extra flavor to the drink.

Lemons and Oranges:
These are cut in half and then sliced four to five times perpendicular to the original half cut. Some bartenders place a small incision in the middle of the fruit so it can straddle the rim of the drink; this is

optional. Oranges are simply squeezed over the drink then dropped in the drink. Lemons are either squeezed over the drink then dropped in, or requested as a "twist." If a twist of lemon is requested, the meat is removed from a portion of the peel and discarded. The portion of peel should be at least an inch long by approximately a quarter inch wide. This piece, referred to as a "twist," is then twisted over the drink and dropped into it. If time permits, rub the twist over the rim of the glass; this will impart more of the peel's flavor to the drink.

Celery Stalks:

These simply need to be cleaned prior to placing in the drink; they are most frequently added to Bloody Marys.

Maraschino Cherries:

These are added to a drink straight from the jar.

Green Pitted Olives and Cocktail Onions:

These are rarely used in anything but Martinis. They are added straight from the jar. A Martini with a cocktail onion is called a Gibson.

It should be noted that on a busy night a bartender will not have time to squeeze every piece of fruit prior to dropping it into the drink.

Large Rocks or Highball Glass.

(10–12 ounces): Always filled with ice, this glass is used for serving most drinks that contain fruit juice or sour mix as primary mixers. The large rocks glass is the most versatile glass. It is used for serving all soft drinks and can be used interchangeably with the Collins glass. The large rocks or highball glass is also used if someone orders a tall drink, for instance a tall Rum and Coke, which is normally served in a small rocks glass.

Small Rocks or Old-Fashioned Glass

(6–10 ounces): Always filled with ice, this glass is used for serving most drinks that contain cola and other sodas, tonic water, water, cream, and sometimes juices as its primary mixers. A small rocks glass is also used for all drinks ordered "on the rocks."

Collins Glass

(10–14 ounces): This glass is used for all drinks ordered "Collins" (desired liquor, sour mix, splash of soda, and a cherry). The Collins glass is also used on select other drinks. The Collins glass is basically interchangeable with the large rocks glass, however it is not as prevalent as the large rocks glass.

Cocktail or Martini Glass

(3–6 ounces): This glass is used for drinks ordered "straight up, chilled" and is most closely associated with the Martini served straight up. If time permits, always chill the cocktail glass before serving a drink in it. The stem of the cocktail glass is to be held by the drinker so as not to warm the contents of the glass. The frappé is the only drink which calls for ice, shaved or crushed, to be added to a cocktail glass.

Whiskey Sour Glass

(4–8 ounces): This glass is used primarily for "sours" (desired liquor, sour mix, a cherry, and a lemon slice) served straight up, chilled. Most other drinks served in sour glasses contain sour mix as their primary mixer.

Brandy Snifter

(Snifter) (4–24 ounces): This glass is used for serving brandy and liqueurs requested "straight up, un-chilled" (straight-up liqueurs can also be served in a cordial glass). The body of the snifter is designed to be held by the palm of the hand, thus warming the snifter's contents.

Shot Glass

($^3/_4$–2 ounces): The shot glass is used exclusively for serving shots.

Cordial

(1–1$^1/_2$ ounces): This glass, sometimes referred to as a "pony," is used for serving liqueurs or cor-dials straight up. The cordial is most often used for after-dinner drinks.

Irish Coffee Cup

(8–12 ounces): This cup is used for serving all hot drinks.

Margarita Glass

(8–14 ounces): This goblet is used for serving frozen drinks, most notably the Frozen Margarita. Margarita glasses are expensive and fragile; for these reasons they are not found behind most bars.

Beer Mug

(10–16 ounces): The mug is the most informal of all beer glasses. The mug is the best glass to chill because its thickness enables it to stay cold longer than any other glass.

Pilsner Glass

(10–14 ounces): This is the most formal beer glass. Because of its fragile nature, this glass is seldom found in bars, but many microbreweries and upscale restaurants have them.

Pint Glass

(14–16 ounces): Today's popular pint glass is a misnomer, in actuality it is usually less than 16 ounces (⅞ of a pint to a pint). It is found at most bars and is used for premium draft beer including ales, porters, and stouts. Due to the popularity of this glass, many bars are beginning to serve more than just beer in the pint glass; in some instances it is being used in place of the large rocks glass.

White Wine Glass

(10–14 ounces): This glass is used for serving white wines and is usually taller than the red wine glass (it has a longer stem, but a smaller lip and bowl).

Red Wine Glass

(12–16 ounces): This glass has a large lip and a large bowl to enable the drinker to experience the aroma and body of the red wine.

Champagne Flute

(6–10 ounces): This glass is used for serving champagne, sparkling wine, and a select few other drinks. The tall and slender glass is designed to show off the wine's sparkling bubbles. Most bars stock only a few of these fragile glasses, because champagne is rarely ordered except for New Year's Eve, at which time most bars serve champagne in less-expensive plastic flutes.

Punch Cup

(6–8 ounces): This glass is generally not found behind bars, but rather at parties where eggnog and punch are served.

TOOLS OF
THE BAR

Jigger/Pony:

This nonregulated measuring instrument is referred to in the bar business simply as a "jigger." Each jigger has two sides, a jigger and a pony. The jigger side is usually $\frac{1}{2}$ ounce larger than the pony side. Jiggers come in several different sizes with the jigger side ranging from 1 to 2 ounces and the pony side ranging in size from $\frac{1}{2}$ to 1 ounce. Generally, nightclubs and large bars catering to a younger crowd will have smaller shots and therefore use a smaller jigger than those of country clubs or bars catering to an older clientele.

Shaker:

This instrument is used for shaking or stirring a drink with ice before pouring it into a serving glass. The Boston shaker is found behind most bars. It is a combination large steel tumbler (about 16 ounces) and smaller mixing glass (about 12 ounces). To begin the process, ice is added to the tumbler followed by the drink's ingredients. A drink that needs stirring before being served straight up, is done so at this time then strained into its proper glass. A drink that needs to be shaken is done so by placing the smaller mixing glass into the tumbler creating a water-tight seal. The drink is shaken a few times and then with the tumbler right side up, the mixing glass is removed from the tumbler. The tumbler now has the entire mix including the ice. A strainer is placed over the mouth of the tumbler and the drink is poured into the glass. Gaining a great deal of popu-

larity is a device called a "short shaker." It saves time when making shaken drinks served on the rocks. The short shaker fits over the mouth of the glass the drink will be served in, therefore allowing the drink to be shaken and served in the same glass.

Strainer:

This porous instrument is used in conjunction with a shaker for pouring straight-up drinks chilled. The strainer is placed over the mouth of the shaker when poured. This allows the drink to flow while holding the ice in the shaker. This instrument is used for making any type of chilled drinks including shots and straight-up drinks.

Speedpourer:

This small plastic or metal device fits over the mouth of a bottle and regulates the flow of the bottle's liquid. If you plan to free pour, this device is a must. When placing a speedpourer on a bottle, make sure the device's spout is perpendicular to the bottle's label. This is important for two reasons: first, if you place each speedpourer accordingly on each bottle and keep it in the speed rack with the device's spout facing forward, you can begin pouring immediately without having to check its positioning (it will not pour at an even rate unless it is positioned correctly); second, placing the speedpourer perpendicular to the label will allow the customer to see the label of the bottle while the bartender pours from the bottle.

Bar Spoon:

This spoon has a long handle (usually at least ten inches long) and is used for mixing drinks in all glasses and tumblers.

Blender:

A must for making frozen and ice-cream drinks, as well as blending fresh fruit. If the blender has a strong motor and sharp blades it can also be used for making shaved ice.

Bartender's Friend:

This handy device has all the different tools needed for opening beer and wine bottles.

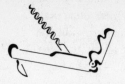

Paring Knife:

Used for cutting garnishes and skinning lemons to create a twist. A sharp paring knife is a must behind the bar.

LIQUOR, LIQUEUR, AND MIXERS

Although it is preferable that the bartender have a strong grasp of the different liquors behind the bar, it is not a necessity. The most important knowledge a bartender should have regarding liquor is the category or class of each brand. Often a patron will request the bartender to list the brands of a certain type of liquor the bar carries. For example, many patrons will ask the bartender what kinds of Scotch (whisky) they have. In this instance the bartender should know what brands of Scotch whisky the bar carries (and which it does not!). Liquors that have a strong "brand following" are: brandy, gin, vodka, and all types of whiskey.

DIVISIONS OF LIQUOR

In all bars there are at least two divisions of liquors: "bar" and "call." Many bars have a third division referred to as "top shelf" or "premium." The first and most inexpensive liquor is "bar" or "well." One step up in quality and price from "bar" liquor is "call" liquor, and this is followed by "top shelf" liquor, the finest and most expensive liquor in the house.

BAR OR WELL LIQUOR

This is the "house" or "no-name" liquor, the cheap stuff. It is used whenever a patron makes no distinction as to the brand of liquor he or she desires. Bar or well liquor is almost always found in metal speed racks behind the bar, in front of the bartender. These racks are usually about three feet above the floor. The location of the racks makes the liquor very accessible. The liquor is also arranged in a set order within the racks to make locating the desired bottle as easy as possible. The following liquor is usually present in a speed rack in this order from right to left:

vodka, American whiskey, gin, rum, tequila, triple sec, and Scotch whisky. Other liquors considered "bar," though not usually located in the speed racks because of their infrequent use, are usually located on shelves behind the bar. These would commonly include liqueurs or cordials such as: amaretto, anisette, curaçao, sloe gin, crème de drinks, and schnapps. Remember, the above list of bar liqueurs is not set in stone. Some bars may have one or two of the above liqueurs in the call section.

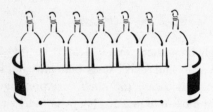

CALL LIQUOR

This is the title given to liquor above bar but below top-shelf liquor in price and quality. Here you will find brand-name American whiskies, mid-range name-brand Scotch whiskies, Irish whiskies, American brandies, most brand-name rums and tequilas, brand-name schnapps such as Rumple Minze, and liqueurs such as Southern Comfort, Jägermeister, and Irish cream. Remember, call and top-shelf liquors are not to be used unless specified by the patron or the drink order.

TOP-SHELF LIQUOR

This class of liquor is proudly displayed behind the bar on attractive, often illuminated, top shelves. The finest and most expensive liquors such as cognac as well as the bar's best bottles of Scotch, vodka, gin, and proprietary liqueurs will be on the top shelf.

The following list contains a concise explanation of the different liquors and their top call brands.

Brandy:

The process used to make brandy is basically the same as that of making whiskey. The difference between the two classes of liquors is that brandy is distilled from fruit while whiskey is derived from grain. Any fruit which is fermented and then distilled is a brandy. The finest brandies are from the Cognac and Armagnac regions of France, although California produces fine brandies as well. Brandy bottles have special labeling to distinguish between the different classes of brandy. For instance, a bottle of brandy with the acronym VSOP on its label describes its contents as Very Special Old Pale. Letters are used in place of words to classify the given bottle. They are:

C—cognac	E—especially
F—fine	O—old
P—pale	S—special
V—very	X—extra

The most popular call brands are: Rémy Martin (Cognac); Hennessy (Cognac); Courvoisier (Cognac); E&J Brandy (American); Christian Brothers (American).

Gin:

This neutral grain spirit is made from juniper berries and an assorted mix of herbs and spices. Gin is normally the second most popular bottle in the speed rack (vodka is the most popular). These two liquors lead the way because they are neutral grain spirits lacking any strong tastes, which make them very mixable. The most popular include Bombay Sapphire, Tanqueray, and Beefeater.

Rum:

First produced in the Caribbean, rum is made from sugar cane and comes in two main classes. *Light rums* are less flavorful and range in color from clear to gold. *Dark rums* are more syrupy and have a richer flavor. Also popular are *flavored rums* like spiced rum and coconut rum. Rum is usually the third most popular bottle in the speed rack. Top-call rums include Myers's (dark), Bacardi (light), Captain Morgan's (spiced), and Malibu (coconut-flavored).

Tequila:

Made in and around the town of Tequila in Mexico, this liquor has gained great popularity over the last twenty-five years. It is made from the *agave tequilana* or blue agave plant. It has a very distinctive, pungent taste. Tequila is a very popular shot and is almost always accompanied with salt and lime (lick salt, drink shot, suck lime), so it's important that you always ask the patron if he or she would like salt and a lime when a tequila shot is ordered. Clear tequilas are usually the bar or well brands. Better tequilas will be darker in color, signifying a longer aging process. Top-call tequilas include José Cuervo and Sauza.

Vodka:

This neutral grain spirit is almost always the most popular "bar" liquor because it can be mixed with almost anything. Although most vodkas have only a smidgen of taste, many today are being produced with mild flavoring, including citrus fruits, pepper, etcetera. Top-call vodkas include Stolichnaya, Tanqueray Sterling, Absolut, and Smirnoff.

Whiskey:

Liquors of this class are made by distilling grains like rye, corn, and barley. Though there are several different classes of whiskies, only origin and consistency will be discussed below. Straight whiskies are those whiskies which are not blended in any way. They are made by one distiller, and because of government regulations are held in bonded warehouses until the barrels of whiskey are bottled. Blended whiskies have no such regulations and, as the name implies, contain the whiskies of two or more distillers blended together. Country of origin is the only other distinction that will be discussed in this book. Each of the four major whiskey-producing countries uses ingredients, distilling processes, even spellings peculiar to its national origin. As a result, each type of whiskey is consumed differently. American and Canadian whiskies are enjoyed neat (straight shots) and are very mixable. Scotch whisky is usually preferred on the rocks or with water, and Irish whiskey is usually enjoyed either on the rocks, as a shot, or with coffee.

AMERICAN WHISKEY: The great majority of this whiskey is distilled in Kentucky, Tennessee, and other bordering states. American whiskey is the most robust of all whiskies, and it is either straight or blended. Of the straight American whiskies there are three major types: bourbon, rye, and corn. **Bourbon whiskey** is by far the most popular. It is made with at least 51 percent corn, the rest being barley and rye.

Rye whiskey is made with at least 51 percent rye with the balance consisting of corn and barley. **Corn whiskey** is the least produced of the three and contains 80 percent corn and the rest a combination of rye and barley. Only those straight whiskies distilled in Bourbon County, Kentucky, can be labeled "bourbon." Some patrons may expect true bourbon when ordering bourbon without distinguishing a name brand, others simply want bar whiskey. Top bar brands include but are not limited to Jim Beam (bourbon), Wild Turkey (straight), Early Times (blended), Jack Daniel's (blended), and Seagram's 7 (blended).

CANADIAN WHISKY: Whiskies of Canada are blended, usually of the rye variety. These whiskies are usually lighter in body and smoother than American whiskey. Top-call Canadian whiskies include Crown Royal, Canadian Club, Seagram's V.O., and Canadian Mist.

IRISH WHISKEY: Arguably the oldest of all (Ireland's Bushmills distilling house dates back to 1608, making it the oldest distiller in the world), Irish whiskey is a blend of grain whiskies and barley malt whiskies giving it a full barley flavor with a lot of bite. Irish whiskey is popular as a neat shot as well as in the famous Irish Coffee. Top-call Irish whiskies include Bushmills and Jameson.

SCOTCH WHISKY: Simply called "Scotch," whiskies of this origin are legendary for their peaty smoothness and smoky flavor. Their unique flavor is derived in great part from the process by which the malt barley is dried over peat fires. Scotch is made in both the straight and blended varieties, and all blends contain grain and malt whiskies. The top whiskies of Scotland are of the single malt or straight type. This class of whiskey has many ardent fans. This is part due to the fact that Scotch is rarely mixed with anything except water, so its taste is very discernible. The most popular mass-produced call brands of Scotch include Glenlivet (single malt/straight), Glenfiddich (single malt/straight), Johnnie Walker (blended), Chivas Regal (blended), Dewar's White Label (blended), J&B (blended), and Cutty Sark (blended).

Liqueurs or cordials, as they are often called, are for the most part sweeter than liquors. They can be divided into several different broad categories though most taste either fruity, nutty, or minty.

Amaretto:
This almond-flavored liqueur is very popular with younger drinkers, especially women. Amaretto is often mixed with sweet and sour mix and/or orange juice. Amaretto di Saronno is the most popular brand-name amaretto.

Anisette:
This liqueur, which tastes like licorice, is seldom ordered, but when ordered is usually requested straight chilled.

Bénédictine*:
This herb-based liqueur is popular among older drinkers. It is usually served straight up, or on the rocks with brandy and called a "B&B." Due to the popularity of the B&B, the Bénédictine company combined the two ingredients in a bottle appropriately named "B&B," which can be found behind most bars.

Cacao, Crème de:
This chocolate-flavored liqueur comes in both dark and white versions.

Campari*:

This bright red liqueur is popular throughout Europe, especially Italy, where it is made, and it is catching on in the States. Campari tastes like quinine (tonic water) and is usually served either on the rocks or mixed with soda water or tonic water.

Cassis, Crème de:

This liqueur is made from black currants, a sweet-tasting berry. It's used in the Sex on the Beach shot/drink, very popular among young adults, as well as in a Kir, where it is combined with white wine.

Chambord*:

This sweet-tasting French liqueur is made primarily from black raspberries, fruit, and honey. It's popularity is growing, especially as an ingredient in specialty shots.

Chartreuse*:

This rich and aromatic herbal liqueur made by Carthusian monks since 1605 comes in two different versions, yellow and green. Over 130 herbs and spices are aged to create this unique looking and tasting liqueur.

Cointreau*:

This is the best-known brand name of triple sec. Though triple sec is present in many drinks as a secondary mixer, Cointreau is seldom "called" in these drinks, though at times ordered straight up.

Curaçao:

This orange-flavored liqueur comes in many colors, but usually blue or orange. It can be used in place of triple sec, or to add color to a drink.

Drambuie*:

Made from Scotch and heather honey, this liqueur is a popular after-dinner drink, and when combined with Scotch makes a Rusty Nail.

Frangelico*:

This hazelnut-flavored liqueur is seldom served but it is used in the Russian Quaalude, a popular drink on the rocks or as a shot.

Galliano*:

This yellow Italian liqueur which comes in the tall thin bottle is sweet and spicy. It is seldom used except for Harvey Wallbangers and the occasional mixed shot.

Grand Marnier*:

The most popular proprietary orange-flavored liqueur. Grand Marnier is not technically a triple sec; it is more closely associated with curaçao, however, it (as any orange-flavored liqueur) can be used instead of triple sec. Grand Marnier is frequently ordered straight up.

Irish Cream:

This sweet-tasting and very rich liqueur made from Irish whiskey and cream has recently become very popular. It is often served on the rocks and is enjoyed in many a shot. There are many quality proprietary liqueurs in this class, the most famous of which is Baileys.

Irish Mist*:

This liqueur, similar to Drambuie in that it is made from whiskey, though Irish, and heather honey, is sweet tasting and very popular served as a shot or straight up on St. Patrick's Day.

Jägermeister*:

This mint-flavored liqueur (technically a bitter) is very popular among young adults. It is almost exclusively ordered as a shot, chilled.

Kahlúa*:
This most popular coffee-flavored liqueur from Mexico is most often used in shots, as well as in both White and Black Russians.

Maraschino:
A sweet cherry liqueur, technically a brandy, which is infrequently used, and then, usually in small quantities.

Menthe, Crème de:
This sweet minty liqueur comes in either green or clear, although the taste is the same. Crème de menthe is used in the Grasshopper, the Stinger, and the Irish Coffee, as well as the occasional after-dinner drink. Green crème de menthe has also found its niche as a dessert topping for vanilla ice cream.

Midori*:
This proprietary brand of melon liqueur is green in color and tastes like a combination between watermelon and cantaloupe. It is used in many of the newer mixed drinks and shots.

Noyau, Crème de:
An almond-flavored liqueur which is seldom used except for the occasional mixed drink or shot.

Ouzo:
This national drink of Greece is anise-based (tastes like licorice) and is ordered often as a shot, chilled.

Pernod*:
A proprietary licorice-flavored absinthe liqueur from France.

Sake:
This unique Japanese drink is brewed from fermented rice, though because of its high alcohol content and taste it is usually thought of as a wine or a liqueur. Technically it is a beer. Most bars do not have sake because it is very rarely ordered, but many Japanese restaurants carry it.

Sambuca:
This licorice-flavored Italian liqueur is very popular served as a chilled shot. It is translucent and colorless, but achieves a cloudy appearance when chilled.

Schnapps:
This category of light and flavorful liqueurs is becoming more and more popular in America. Schnapps flavors include the ever-popular peppermint as well as many new flavors such as root beer, cinnamon, cola, peach, butterscotch, and more.

Sloe Gin:
This sweet-tasting, fruity liqueur made from sloe berries is used in the frequently ordered and aptly named Sloe Gin Fizz.

Southern Comfort*:
This peach-flavored American liqueur is popular served as a shot, or in mixed drinks such as the Alabama Slammer.

Tia Maria*:
This coffee-flavored liqueur is made from rum and spices. It is often used in shots, less often as an after-dinner drink on the rocks.

Triple Sec:
This orange-flavored liqueur is a very common

---

ingredient in mixed drinks. The most popular proprietary brand is Cointreau.

Vermouth:

This spirit, technically a wine, comes in two types, dry and sweet. Unlike most other liqueurs, vermouth will become stale if left unrefrigerated at length after opening. *Dry vermouth* is extremely strong tasting. It is used in the making of Martinis, and due to its strong taste a Dry Martini should only contain a few drops. *Sweet vermouth* is, as its name implies, sweet. It is used in the Manhattan and is at times ordered on the rocks.

Yukon Jack*:

This strong Canadian whisky– based liqueur has citrus and herb flavors and is served as a neat shot or in specialty shots such as the Jackhammer.

*Denotes those liqueurs which are proprietary (brand name), all others are classes of liquor.

BEER

Brewed and fermented cereal grains are the most ancient of all alcoholic beverages, dating back to 7000 B.C. The predominant cereal used in the production of beer is barley, which is roasted then combined with other cereal grains and cooked with water. The liquid residue of this process is called wort, which is then extracted, combined with hops, and boiled in a kettle. The hops are then removed, and yeast is added, as the catalyst in the fermentation process. The yeast consumes the malt sugar, the by-product of which is alcohol. Beer should be stored in a cool, dry place away from any direct light, especially sunlight.

Ale:

This top-fermented brew is growing in popular-

ity. It originated in Britain, and is now being produced with great success by the micro-breweries of
North America. Ale is a full-bodied beer with a
strong taste of hops. It ranges in color from a deep
copper to pale lighter ales, which approach the almost clear appearance of a lager.

Bock:
This class of beer first produced in Germany is a
stronger (6 to 13 percent alcohol) and more full-
bodied class of lager beer. It is also a seasonal beer
produced in both the spring and fall.

Creme Ale:
A combination of ale and lager are blended together to create this highly carbonated beer.

Lager:
This beer is what most people drink when they
simply order a "beer" or "light beer." All of the mass-
produced American beers are lagers, as are most of
the beers produced in the world. Lager is produced
via bottom fermentation, the youngest of beer-pro-
duction processes, which creates a clear-bodied
beer with more stability and effervescence; however, to the lovers of the older methods of production, taste and character are lost in beers produced
by this method.

Malt Liquor:
This American beer has a great deal of variation in
taste and color. The color can range from light to
dark, and the flavor can range from very subtle to very
hoppy. The alcohol content of malt liquor is higher
than that of most beers, generally over 5 percent.

Pilsner:
This bottom-fermented beer is light golden in

color and has a crisp, clean taste. Pilsner derives its name from the Bohemian city of Pilsen where this type of beer was first brewed.

Porter:
This top-fermented ale is very bitter. Porter is full-bodied and rich, very similar to stout in most aspects, though not as strong.

Stout:
This darkest of beers is very creamy and strong. It is most commonly associated with the British Isles where the most well-known stout, Guinness, of Ireland is made.

Weisse Beer:
As with other beers, this type of beer is brewed with barley. However, unique to weisse beer is that a percentage of wheat is also added. If a bar offers weisse beer it should have large pilsner glasses, sometimes referred to as weisse beer glasses because those who drink this type of beer usually request a large slice of lemon to add to the drink.

WINE

Produced from the fermentation of grapes, wine dates back over six thousand years. After harvesting the grape, primarily in the fall when the grape is at its ripest, the fruit is crushed and pressed to remove all stems and skin. The juice is then placed in a vat and allowed to ferment under the influence of natural grape yeast. When this process is complete, the resulting wine is aged in casks. Only after the wine has been sufficiently aged is it ready for bottling.

There are a myriad of different grapes used in the production of wine. Knowing the variety of grape will give the connoisseur a rough idea of the characteristics of that wine. Although one variety of grape may be grown in several different regions of the world, each will contain certain characteristics inherent to that region. The variety of grape is, however, only one factor in the formation of wine. The vineyard soil, climate, and the techniques employed in production can have a greater effect on the wine than even the grape's variety. The final variable in the making of wine is its vintage, or year in which it was produced. Certain climatic and atmospheric conditions as well as mold, rot, and pests can have great impact on the quality of the grape, affecting the wine it will produce.

The varieties of grape number in the thousands. However, there are only a few varieties which, due to their outstanding characteristics, have been selected by winemakers for cultivation in many regions of the world. Most of the varieties have their origins in the vineyards of Europe. Some of the most popular white wines are derived from the following grape varieties: Chablis, Chardonnay, Chenin Blanc, Fumé Blanc, Sauvignon Blanc, and Riesling. Some of the most popular red wines are derived from the following grape varieties: Burgundy, Cabernet Sauvignon, Chianti, Merlot, Pinot Noir, and Zinfandel.

MIXERS

Bitters:
This bitter-tasting mixer, which contains alcohol, has seen a steady decline in its use over the past few decades. Though called for in many drinks, bitters are often omitted. There are many different types of bitters. Angostura bitters are the most popular and are found behind most bars. A few drops of Angostura bitters will give any drink a strong taste. A popular bartender's myth for curing hiccups is a glass of soda water and a dash of bitters.

Club Soda or Soda Water:

This is simply carbonated water. This mixer is located in the soda gun, if the bar is equipped with one.

Cream:

In the past, heavy or whipping cream was used in the making of many drinks. Today regular cream has replaced heavy cream. Cream is lighter than heavy cream and therefore allows the drinker to consume more drinks before feeling full.

Grenadine:

This sweet red syrup made from pomegranates is used in small quantities in many drinks. It is usually contained in a 12-ounce bottle.

Lime Juice:

This mixer is used in small doses in many drinks. Rose's is the most popular brand. It usually comes in a 12-ounce bottle.

Sour Mix:

Also called "sweet and sour mix," it's a combination of lemon juice, lime juice, and sugar. This mixer is used in many drinks including Collinses, Fizzes, Margaritas, and, of course, Sours. Sour mix is either found in large plastic mixing bottles in the bar's speed rack or in the soda gun.

Tonic Water:

This mixer is flavored with lemon, lime, and quinine. Tonic water is almost always found in the soda gun (its button is usually Q for quinine).

AMERICA'S MOST POPULAR DRINKS

When giving recipes to mixed drinks, the other guides list the calculated measurement of each ingredient as if each drink were to be made with a measuring cup, a tablespoon, and a teaspoon. This is not how mixing drinks should be done. Bartending is an art, not a science, and for that reason the bartender must learn to use the tools at his or her disposal. A measuring cup and measuring spoons do not fall into this category. In a perfect world, drink recipes given in ounces would be fine, but behind a busy bar this is not possible. This is impossible for two reasons: first, the bar environment rarely leaves the bartender enough time to slowly and carefully measure each ingredient as the other guides would have you do. More importantly, liquor measurements should be given with regard to the shot because this measurement is determined by the given bar and not by the bartending guide. Even in the comfort of your own home, who wants to measure every ingredient precisely before adding it to a drink.

The system which *The Perfect Cocktail* employs is not only based on the shot glass, but also the bar glass. Using the correct bar glass insures that the ingredients including the mixers will be properly regulated. The secondary mixer is usually such a small amount, usually a splash or a dash, it can be estimated by the bartender. Primary mixers are listed without any measurement at all, but you should remember some drinks have more than one primary mixer. If more than one primary mixer is required, add equal parts of each. When pouring primary mixers, fill the glass up leaving a little more than half an inch at the rim. This space is to avert spillage or for the secondary mixers if they have yet to be added to the drink. If a drink has the option of being served straight up, ounces will be given for the drink's ingredients. This is because straight-up drinks are made in a shaker, and so cannot be regulated by the glass in which they are served. If the drink is to be served on the rocks, disregard the ounces in the recipe and simply serve in the appropriate glass. In all drinks other than those which can be ordered "straight up," secondary mixers will be the only part of the recipe given as ounces, a splash, or a dash. A splash is a little less than ½ ounce, a dash is several drops. This system is very easy to learn and allows the bartender to work quickly while keeping his or her mind from being cluttered with measurements that are better regulated by the bar glass.

Next to each recipe is an illustration of the type of glass used. Some of the drinks include two glasses, often a small rocks glass and a cocktail glass. Whenever these two glasses appear with a drink recipe, it means that the given drink can either be served on the rocks or straight up, chilled. If someone orders one of these drinks, you should ask how they want their drink, straight up or on the rocks. The reason for the two glasses is that these drinks were originally intended to be chilled and served straight up in a cocktail glass. Today, the trend is toward serving these drinks on the rocks in a small rocks glass. In most cases, the first glass depicted should be your first choice in which to serve the drink, but either is appropriate. There are other drinks, such as Sours and Margaritas, which have a choice of glasses based on how the drink is to be served. The description of each glass in the chapter entitled "Bar Glasses" will give you a better understanding of when each glass is to be used.

ALABAMA SLAMMER

- ¾ shot amaretto
- ¾ shot Southern Comfort
- Splash of sloe gin
- Orange juice
- Pineapple juice

Stir.

AMARETTO SOUR

- 1 shot amaretto
- Sour mix
- Orange slice

Shake and garnish.

AMARETTO STONE SOUR

- 1 shot amaretto
- Sour mix
- Orange juice
- Orange slice

Shake and garnish.

BAY BREEZE

- 1 shot vodka
- Pineapple juice
- Cranberry juice

Stir.

BLACK RUSSIAN

- 1 shot vodka
- ½ shot coffee-flavored liqueur (Kahlúa)

Stir.

BLOODY MARY

- 1 shot vodka
- Tomato juice

- Splash of lemon juice
- Dash of Worcestershire sauce
- Dash of Tabasco sauce
- Sprinkle of celery salt or pepper
- Celery stalk or lime wedge

Garnish and serve.

BLUE HAWAIIAN

- ½ shot rum
- ½ shot blue curaçao
- ½ shot crème de coconut
- Pineapple juice
- Cherry

Blend with ice and garnish.

BRANDY ALEXANDER

- ½ shot brandy
- ½ shot crème de cacao (dark)
- Splash of cream

Shake.

CAPE CODDER

- 1 shot vodka
- Cranberry juice
- Lime wedge

Stir and garnish.

CUBA LIBRE

- 1 shot rum
- Cola
- Splash of lime juice
- Lime wedge

Garnish and serve.

DAIQUIRI

- 1 shot rum
- Splash of lime juice
- 1 teaspoon/packet sugar

Shake.

FRAPPÉ

- 1 shot any liqueur

Pour liqueur over shaved/crushed ice in a champagne flute or cocktail glass. Serve.

FROZEN DAIQUIRI

- 1 shot rum
- Splash of triple sec
- 1 ounce lime juice
- 1 teaspoon/packet sugar

Blend with ice.

FUZZY NAVEL

- 1 shot peach schnapps
- Orange juice
- Orange slice

Garnish and serve.

GIMLET

- 1 shot gin
- ¾ ounce lime juice
- Lime wedge

Stir.

GIN AND TONIC

- 1 shot gin
- Tonic water
- Lime wedge

Garnish and serve.

GRASSHOPPER

- ½ shot crème de menthe (green)
- ½ shot crème de cacao (white)
- ¾ ounce cream

Shake.

GREYHOUND/SALTY DOG

- 1 shot vodka
- Grapefruit juice

stir. (Salty Dog: Salt rim of glass.)

IRISH COFFEE

- 1 shot Irish whiskey
- Black coffee to within ½ inch of rim
- 1 teaspoon/packet sugar
- Whipped cream, topped with a splash of crème de menthe (green)

Serve.

HARVEY WALLBANGER

- ¾ shot vodka
- Orange juice
- ¼ shot Galliano, floated on top

Serve.

KAMIKAZE

- ¾ shot vodka
- ¾ shot triple sec
- ¾ ounce lime juice

Shake.

KIR

- 3 ounces white wine
- Splash of crème de cassis
- Lemon twist

Pour over ice and garnish. (Lemon twist is optional but most bartenders include it. Do not stir.)

LONG ISLAND ICED TEA

- ½ shot vodka
- ½ shot gin
- ½ shot rum
- ½ shot tequila
- Splash of triple sec
- Sour mix
- Splash of cola
- Lemon slice

Garnish and serve.

LYNCHBURG LEMONADE

- 1 shot Jack Daniel's
- Splash of triple sec
- Sour mix
- Lemon-lime soda
- Lemon slice

Garnish and serve.

MADRAS

- 1 shot vodka
- Orange juice
- Cranberry juice
- Lime wedge

Garnish and serve.

MAI TAI

- ½ shot rum
- ½ shot dark rum
- ¼ shot curaçao
- Splash of grenadine
- Splash of lime juice
- Splash of orgeat (almond syrup)
- Cherry

Shake.

MANHATTAN

- 1 shot blended whiskey
- ½ shot sweet vermouth
- Cherry

Stir and garnish.

PERFECT MANHATTAN

- 1 shot blended whiskey
- Dash of sweet vermouth
- Dash of dry vermouth
- Cherry

Stir and garnish.

Prior to making a Margarita ask the patron two important questions:

1. Would you like the rim salted? If you are unable to ask, salt the rim.

2. Would you like it straight up, on the rocks, or frozen?

A Margarita straight up is served in a cocktail glass.

A Margarita on the rocks is served in either a small rocks glass or a Margarita glass.

A Frozen Margarita is served in a stemmed goblet, either a Margarita glass, Whiskey Sour glass, or large wineglass.

MARGARITA

Salt rim (if desired).

- 1 shot tequila
- ¼ shot triple sec
- Sour mix
- Splash of lime juice
- Lime wedge (on request)

Shake. For Frozen Margarita, blend with ice.

GOLDEN MARGARITA

Salt rim (if desired)

- 1 shot José Cuervo 1800 tequila or other premium gold tequila
- ¼ shot Cointreau

- Sour mix
- Splash of orange juice
- Splash of lime juice
- Lime wedge (on request)

Shake to make the Margarita up or on the rocks. Blend with ice for Frozen Margarita. Garnish.

BLUE MARGARITA
Salt rim (if desired)
- 1 shot tequila
- ¼ shot blue curaçao
- Sour mix
- Splash of lime juice

Shake.

STRAWBERRY MARGARITA
Salt rim (if desired)
- 1 shot tequila
- ½ shot strawberry liqueur
- ¼ shot triple sec
- 1 ounce sour mix
- 3 ounces strawberry mix
- Strawberry or lime wedge

Blend with ice and garnish.

MARTINIS

Prior to making a Martini ask the patron four important questions:

1. Will this be a Gin or Vodka Martini? If for some reason you are unable to ask (waitress forgets, too busy, etc.), assume gin.

2. Would you like it straight up or on the rocks? If for some reason you are unable to ask, assume straight up.

3. Would you like it dry? This is an important question and should be asked, if unable to ask, make it dry, vermouth can always be added.

4. Would you like a garnish? Most prefer a twist of lemon, some an olive.

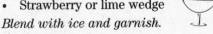

A Gibson is a Martini, usually dry, garnished with a cocktail onion.

MARTINI

If it's on the rocks, add ice.

- 1½ shots gin
- Dash of dry vermouth
- Desired garnish

Stir and garnish.

If it's straight up, fill shaker with ice, and fill with:

- 1½ shots gin
- Dash of dry vermouth
- Desired garnish

Stir and strain into cocktail glass. Garnish.

DRY MARTINI

If it's on the rocks, add ice.

- 1½ shots gin
- ½ dash of dry vermouth
- Desired garnish

Stir and garnish.

If it's straight up, fill shaker with ice and fill with:

- 1½ shots gin
- ½ dash of dry vermouth
- Desired garnish

Stir and strain into cocktail glass. Garnish.

EXTRA DRY MARTINI

Add splash of dry vermouth to either empty rocks glass or cocktail glass, depending on whether drink is ordered "on the rocks" or "straight up." Swish dry vermouth around in empty glass and dump it out.

If it's on the rocks, add ice to small rocks glass.

- 1½ shots gin
- 1–2 drops of dry vermouth

- Desired garnish

Stir and garnish

Straight up, fill shaker with ice. Fill with:

- 1½ shots gin
- 1 drop of dry vermouth
- Desired garnish

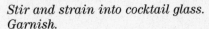

Stir and strain into cocktail glass.
Garnish.

To make an Extra Dry Martini add only 1 or 2 drops of dry vermouth into the Martini. To accomplish this, first place clean index finger over speed pourer and tilt bottle just enough to insure a limited flow of vermouth. Second, release finger from pourer just enough to let 1 or 2 drops into glass. Due to the very strong taste of dry vermouth, 1 or 2 drops will be enough to impart its flavor to the drink without being too overpowering.

MELON BALL

- ½ shot vodka
- ½ shot melon liqueur (Midori)
- Pineapple juice
- Orange slice

Garnish and serve.

OLD-FASHIONED

- 1 shot blended whiskey
- 1 teaspoon/packet sugar
- Dash of bitters
- Dash of water

Stir.

PIÑA COLADA

- 1½ shots rum
- 4 ounces pineapple juice and 2 ounces coconut milk; OR 6 ounces piña colada mix
- Cherry

Blend with ice and garnish.

ROASTED TOASTED ALMOND

- ½ shot amaretto
- ½ shot coffee-flavored liqueur (Kahlúa)
- ½ shot vodka
- Cream

Shake.

ROB ROY

- 1 shot Scotch whisky
- ½ shot sweet vermouth
- Cherry

Stir and garnish.

RUM AND COKE

(A Captain and Coke is a Rum and Coke with Captain Morgan's spiced rum.)

- 1 shot rum
- Cola

Serve.

RUSTY NAIL

- 1 shot Scotch whisky
- ½ shot Drambuie

Stir.

SCREWDRIVER

- 1 shot vodka
- Orange juice

Serve.

SEABREEZE

- 1 shot vodka
- Grapefruit juice
- Cranberry juice
- Lime wedge

Stir and garnish.

7 & 7
- 1 shot Seagram's 7 whiskey
- Lemon-lime soda (7-Up)

Serve.

SEX ON THE BEACH
- ¾ shot crème de cassis
- ¾ shot melon liqueur (Midori)
- Pineapple juice

Serve.

SLOE DRIVER
- 1 shot sloe gin
- Orange juice

Serve.

SLOE GIN FIZZ
- 1 shot sloe gin
- Sour mix
- Splash of soda water
- Cherry

Shake with ice prior to adding soda water.
Garnish.

SLOE SCREW
- ¾ shot vodka
- ¼ shot sloe gin
- Orange juice

Serve.

SPRITZER
- 3 ounces white wine
- Soda water

Serve.

STINGER
- ¾ shot brandy
- ¾ shot crème de menthe (white)

Stir.

STRAWBERRY DAIQUIRI

- 1 shot rum
- ½ shot strawberry liqueur
- 2 ounces strawberry mix or fresh strawberries
- Splash of lime juice

Blend with ice.

TEQUILA SUNRISE

- 1 shot tequila
- Orange juice
- Dash of grenadine

Stir.

TOASTED ALMOND

- ¾ shot amaretto
- ¾ shot coffee-flavored liqueur (Kahlúa)
- Cream

Shake.

TOM COLLINS

- 1 shot gin
- Sour mix
- Splash of soda water
- Cherry and orange slice

Shake with ice prior to adding soda water. Garnish.

VODKA GRASSHOPPER

- ½ shot vodka
- ½ shot crème de menthe (green)
- ½ shot crème de cacao (white)
- Splash of cream

Shake.

VODKA STINGER

- ¾ shot vodka
- ¾ shot crème de menthe (white)

Stir.

VODKA AND TONIC

- 1 shot vodka
- Tonic water
- Lime wedge

Garnish and serve.

WATERMELON

- ½ shot vodka
- ½ shot strawberry liqueur
- Orange juice

Serve.

WHISKEY SOUR

- 1 shot whiskey
- Sour mix
- Cherry and lemon slice

Shake and garnish.

WHITE RUSSIAN

- 1 shot vodka
- ½ shot coffee-flavored liqueur (Kahlúa)
- Cream

Shake.

WOO WOO

- ½ shot vodka
- ½ shot peach schnapps
- Cranberry juice

Stir.

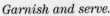

YOUR DRINKS AND NOTES

MIXED SHOTS

This section contains the most extensive list of mixed shots to be found in any book. It should be noted that drink recipes, especially shot recipes, vary from region to region. *The Perfect Cocktail* has made every attempt to use the most widely accepted recipe for each shot.

The ingredients of these mixed shots are not presented in ounces, as in other guides, but rather in fractions of a shot. This is done for two reasons: 1) because each individual bar determines the size of its shot; and 2) because mixed shots are from time to time ordered as mixed drinks. The bartender has a great deal of leeway when making mixed drinks that were originally intended as shots. There are no hard-and-fast rules regarding this aspect of bartending, so it's okay to experiment.

Some of these shots when made as a mixed drink are better tasting when more mixer is used and served in a large rocks glass. Others benefit from not having as much mixer and served in a small rocks glass. If ordered as a mixed drink, a shot that is all liquor, with no mixer, should be served as an on-the-rocks drink (a shot and a half) in a small rocks glass.

ALABAMA SLAMMER
- ⅕ shot amaretto
- ⅕ shot Southern Comfort

- ⅕ shot sloe gin
- ⅕ shot orange juice
- ⅕ shot pineapple juice

Chill in shaker.

ANTIFREEZE

- ½ shot vodka
- ½ shot crème de menthe (green)

Chill.

B-52

- ⅓ shot coffee-flavored liqueur (Kahlúa)
- ⅓ shot Irish cream
- ⅓ shot Grand Marnier

Layer.

BABE RUTH

- ½ shot hazelnut liqueur (Frangelico)
- ½ shot vodka
- A few peanuts

Layer and garnish.

BALD-HEADED WOMAN

- ¾ shot 151-proof rum
- ¼ shot grapefruit juice

Chill.

BARN BURNER

- ½ shot vodka
- ½ shot tomato juice
- Dash of Tabasco sauce

Pour directly into glass.

BETWEEN THE SHEETS

- ⅓ shot brandy
- ⅓ shot triple sec
- ⅓ shot rum
- Dash of lime juice

Chill.

BIKINI LINE

- ⅓ shot vodka
- ⅓ shot Tia Maria
- ⅓ shot Chambord

Chill.

BLACK ORCHID

- ¼ shot rum
- ¼ shot blue curaçao
- ¼ shot grenadine
- ¼ shot cranberry juice
- Dash of lemon-lime soda

Chill.

BLOODY STOOL

- ¼ shot Irish cream
- ¼ shot 151-proof rum
- ¼ shot Campari
- ¼ shot lime juice

Serve.

BLOW JOB

- ⅗ shot Irish cream
- ⅖ shot vodka
- 1–1½ inches of whipped cream for topping

Pour directly into glass, then top. Drinker should bend over and pick shot glass up with his/her mouth, no hands. Take shot down by bending head back and letting shot pour down throat.

BLUE MARLIN

- ¾ shot rum
- ¼ shot blue curaçao
- Dash of lime juice

Chill.

BOILERMAKER

- 1 shot blended whiskey
- 1 mug of beer

This drink can be drunk in any of a number of ways. 1. Shoot the whiskey straight and drink the beer. 2. Pour the whiskey into the beer and drink the mix. 3. Drop the shot, glass and all, into the beer and chug the mix (also called a Depth Charge).

BRAIN

- ¾ shot Irish cream
- ¼ shot peach schnapps

Serve.

BRAIN HEMORRHAGE

- ¾ shot Irish cream
- ¼ shot peach schnapps
- Dash of grenadine

Serve.

BUBBLE GUM

- ¼ shot vodka
- ¼ shot crème de banana
- ¼ shot peach schnapps
- ¼ shot orange juice

Chill.

BUFFALO SWEAT

- ⅓ shot tequila
- ⅓ shot 151-proof rum
- ⅓ shot Tabasco sauce

Serve.

BUTTERY FINGER

- ¼ shot vodka
- ¼ shot Irish cream
- ¼ shot butterscotch schnapps
- ¼ shot coffee-flavored liqueur (Kahlúa)

Chill.

BUTTERY NIPPLE

- ⅓ shot vodka
- ⅓ shot Irish cream
- ⅓ shot butterscotch schnapps

Chill.

BUZZARD'S BREATH

- ⅓ shot amaretto
- ⅓ shot peppermint schnapps
- ⅓ shot coffee-flavored liqueur (Kahlúa)

Chill.

CEMENT MIXER

- ¾ shot Irish cream
- ¼ shot lime juice

Pour directly into glass. Let stand for 30
seconds and drink will coagulate.

CHOCOLATE-COVERED CHERRY

- ⅓ shot amaretto
- ⅓ shot coffee-flavored liqueur (Kahlúa)
- ⅓ shot crème de cacao (white)
- Drop of grenadine

Chill in shaker, pour, then add a drop of
grenadine in center of drink.

COCAINE SHOOTER

- ⅕ shot vodka
- ⅕ shot Chambord
- ⅕ shot Southern Comfort
- ⅕ shot orange juice
- ⅕ shot cranberry juice

Chill.

COMFORTABLE PIRATE

- ¾ shot spiced rum (Captain Morgan's)
- ¼ shot Southern Comfort
- Dash of pineapple juice

Chill.

COOL-AID SHOT

- ¼ shot amaretto
- ¼ shot Southern Comfort
- ¼ shot melon liqueur (Midori)
- ¼ shot cranberry juice

Chill.

CORDLESS SCREWDRIVER

- 1 shot vodka
- 1 teaspoon/packet sugar
- Orange slice

Pour directly into glass. Put sugar half in shot and half on slice of orange, which is placed on rim of shot glass. Drink shot and take a draw on orange.

COSMOS

- 1 shot vodka
- Dash of lime juice

Chill.

COUGH SYRUP

- ½ shot amaretto
- ½ shot Southern Comfort
- Dash of grenadine

Serve.

DIRTY GIRL SCOUT COOKIE

- ⅔ shot Irish cream
- ⅓ shot crème de menthe (green)

Chill.

DR. PIPPER

- ¾ shot amaretto
- ¼ shot 151-proof rum
- 6 ounces beer in separate glass

Chill. Drop shot into beer and drink.

FIREBALL

- ¾ shot cinnamon schnapps
- ¼ shot Tabasco sauce

Serve.

FIRE-BREATHING DRAGON

- ⅓ shot tequila
- ⅓ shot Campari
- ⅓ shot 151-proof rum

Serve.

FOURTH OF JULY

- ⅓ shot grenadine
- ⅓ shot vodka
- ⅓ shot blue curaçao

Layer.

FRENCH CONNECTION

- ½ shot Grand Marnier
- ½ shot cognac

Serve.

FROG LICK

- ⅖ shot vodka
- ⅖ shot Yukon Jack
- ⅕ shot lime juice

Chill.

FUCK ME UP

- ¼ shot cinnamon schnapps
- ¼ shot peppermint schnapps
- ¼ shot Jägermeister
- ¼ shot 151-proof rum

Chill prior to adding rum. Float rum on top.

GRAPE CRUSH

- ½ shot vodka
- ½ shot Chambord
- Dash of sour mix

Serve.

GREEN DEMON

- ¼ shot vodka
- ¼ shot rum
- ¼ shot melon liqueur (Midori)
- ¼ shot sour mix

Chill.

GREEN LIZARD

- ¾ shot Chartreuse (green)
- ¼ shot 151-proof rum

Chill.

HAPPY RANCHER SHOT

- ⅕ shot Scotch whisky
- ⅕ shot peach schnapps
- ⅕ shot melon liqueur (Midori)
- ⅕ shot vodka
- ⅕ shot lemon-lime soda

Chill.

HEAD BANGER

- ½ shot ouzo
- ½ shot 151-proof rum
- Dash of grenadine

Chill.

HONOLULU PUNCH SHOT

- ⅕ shot Southern Comfort
- ⅕ shot 151-proof rum
- ⅕ shot amaretto
- ⅕ shot pineapple juice

- ⅕ shot orange juice
- Dash of grenadine

Chill.

HUMMER

- ½ shot rum
- ¼ shot coffee-flavored liqueur (Kahlúa)
- ¼ shot cream

Serve.

HURRICANE

- ½ shot Jägermeister
- ½ shot Yukon Jack
- Dash of Irish cream

Pour directly into glass, drink will swirl like its namesake.

ILLUSION

- ⅕ shot rum
- ⅕ shot vodka
- ⅕ shot triple sec
- ⅕ shot tequila
- ⅕ shot melon liquor (Midori)
- Dash of lime juice

Chill.

INTERNATIONAL INCIDENT

- ⅕ shot amaretto
- ⅕ shot vodka
- ⅕ shot coffee-flavored liqueur (Kahlúa)
- ⅕ shot hazelnut liqueur (Frangelico)
- ⅕ shot Irish cream

Chill.

IRISH CHARLIE

- ½ shot Irish cream
- ½ shot crème de menthe (white)

Chill.

IRISH FLAG

- ⅓ shot crème de menthe (green)
- ⅓ shot Irish cream
- ⅓ shot Grand Marnier

Layer.

JACKHAMMER

- ¾ shot root beer schnapps
- ¼ shot Yukon Jack

Chill.

JÄGER SHAKE

- ⅕ shot Jägermeister
- ⅕ shot Irish cream
- ⅕ shot root beer schnapps
- ⅕ shot amaretto
- ⅕ shot cola

Chill.

JAWBREAKER

- 1 shot cinnamon schnapps
- Dash of Tabasco

Serve.

GELATIN SHOTS

- 6 ounces desired flavor gelatin mix
- 12 ounces vodka
- 12 ounces boiling water

Mix all ingredients in a pan until gelatin has dissolved. Place in refrigerator. Gelatin Shots can be eaten in the jelled form (like gelatin is traditionally eaten), or drunk like a shot. To drink like a shot, remove the mix from the refrigerator before it has jelled.

JELLY BEAN

- ½ shot anisette
- ½ shot blackberry brandy

Chill.

JELLYFISH

- ¼ shot crème de cacao (white)
- ¼ shot amaretto
- ¼ shot Irish cream
- ¼ shot grenadine

Pour first 3 ingredients directly into glass.
Pour grenadine in center of glass.

KAMIKAZE

- ⅓ shot vodka
- ⅓ shot triple sec
- ⅓ shot lime juice

Chill.

LEMON DROP

- 1 shot vodka
- 1 teaspoon/packet sugar
- Lemon slice

Pour vodka directly into glass. Then half the
sugar in shot and half on slice of lemon,
which is placed on rim of shot glass. Drink
shot and take a draw on lemon.

LETHAL INJECTION

- ⅙ shot spiced rum (Captain Morgan's)
- ⅙ shot Malibu rum
- ⅙ shot crème de noyau
- ⅙ shot rum
- ⅙ shot orange juice
- ⅙ shot pineapple juice

Chill.

LIMP MOOSE

- ½ shot Canadian whisky
- ½ shot Irish cream

Chill.

LION TAMER

- ¾ shot Southern Comfort
- ¼ shot lime juice

Chill.

LIQUID COCAINE

- ⅖ shot peppermint schnapps
- ⅖ shot Jägermeister
- ⅕ shot 151-proof rum

Chill.

LOBOTOMY

- ⅓ shot amaretto
- ⅓ shot Chambord
- ⅓ shot pineapple juice

Chill.

LUNCH PAIL

- ½ shot amaretto
- ½ shot orange juice
- 6 ounces beer in separate glass

Chill.

MELON BALL

- ⅓ shot melon liqueur (Midori)
- ⅓ shot vodka
- ⅓ shot pineapple juice

Chill.

MIND ERASER

Add ice to small rocks glass.

- ⅓ shot coffee-flavored liqueur (Kahlúa)
- ⅓ shot vodka
- ⅓ shot Jack Daniel's
- Splash of soda water
- Large drinking straw

Suck drink down through straw in one gulp.

NUTTY IRISHMAN

- ½ shot Irish cream
- ½ shot hazelnut liqueur (Frangelico)

Chill.

NUTTY PROFESSOR

- ⅓ shot Irish cream
- ⅓ shot hazelnut liqueur (Frangelico)
- ⅓ shot Grand Marnier

Chill.

ORANGE CRUSH

- ½ shot vodka
- ½ shot triple sec
- Dash of soda water

Serve.

ORGASM

- ⅓ shot amaretto
- ⅓ shot coffee-flavored liqueur (Kahlúa)
- ⅓ shot Irish cream

Chill.

ORIENTAL RUG

- ¼ shot Irish cream
- ¼ shot hazelnut liqueur (Frangelico)
- ¼ shot Jägermeister
- ¼ shot coffee-flavored liqueur (Kahlúa)
- Dash of cola

Chill.

PEACH TART

- ¾ shot peach schnapps
- ¼ shot lime juice

Chill.

PEANUT BUTTER AND JELLY

- ½ shot hazelnut liqueur (Frangelico)
- ½ shot Chambord

Serve.

PIGSKIN

- ⅓ shot vodka
- ⅓ shot melon liqueur (Midori)
- ⅓ shot sour mix

Chill.

PINEAPPLE BOMBER

- ⅓ shot Jack Daniel's
- ⅓ shot Southern Comfort
- ⅓ shot pineapple juice

Chill.

PLENTY & GOOD SHOT

- ½ shot ouzo
- ½ shot coffee-flavored liqueur (Kahlúa)

Chill.

POPPERS

- ¾ shot desired liquor
- Splash of lemon-lime soda

Pour desired liquor directly into glass. Place napkin over the top of the shot glass, take the shot glass in the palm of your hand, and slam shot glass down against top of bar or table and immediately drink. This action will cause the lemon-lime soda to fizz, which will mask the taste of the liquor.

PRAIRIE FIRE

- 1 shot tequila
- Dash of Tabasco sauce

Serve.

PURPLE HAZE

Add ice to small rocks glass.

- ²/₅ shot vodka
- ²/₅ shot Chambord
- ¹/₅ shot triple sec
- Splash of lime juice
- Splash of soda water
- Large drinking straw

Suck drink down through straw in one gulp.

PURPLE HOOTER

- ¹/₄ shot Chambord
- ¹/₄ shot vodka
- ¹/₄ shot sour mix
- ¹/₄ shot lemon-lime soda

Chill.

RED DEATH

- ¹/₅ shot amaretto
- ¹/₅ shot sloe gin
- ¹/₅ shot Southern Comfort
- ¹/₅ shot vodka
- ¹/₅ shot triple sec
- Dash of orange juice
- Dash of grenadine

Chill.

RED DRAGON

- ¹/₂ shot tequila
- ¹/₂ shot Campari

Chill.

ROAD KILL

- ¹/₃ shot Irish whiskey
- ¹/₃ shot Wild Turkey whiskey
- ¹/₃ shot 151-proof rum

Chill.

ROCKY MOUNTAIN

- ½ shot amaretto
- ½ shot Southern Comfort
- Dash of lime juice

Chill.

ROOT BEER

- ¼ shot Galliano
- ¼ shot coffee-flavored liqueur (Kahlúa)
- ¼ shot vodka
- ¼ shot cola

Chill.

RUSSIAN QUAALUDE

- ⅕ shot Stolichnaya (or other Russian vodka)
- ⅖ shot hazelnut liqueur (Frangelico)
- ⅖ shot amaretto

Chill.

SAMBUCA SLIDE

- ½ shot sambuca
- ¼ shot vodka
- ¼ shot cream

Chill.

SCOOTER

- ½ shot amaretto
- ½ shot brandy
- Dash of cream

Chill.

SCREAMING ORGASM

- ¼ shot vodka
- ¼ shot coffee-flavored liqueur (Kahlúa)
- ¼ shot Irish cream
- ¼ shot amaretto

Chill.

SEX ON THE BEACH

- ²/₅ shot crème de cassis
- ²/₅ shot melon liqueur (Midori)
- ¹/₅ shot pineapple juice

Chill.

SILK PANTIES

- ¹/₂ shot vodka
- ¹/₂ shot peach schnapps

Chill.

SILVER SPIDER

- ¹/₄ shot vodka
- ¹/₄ shot rum
- ¹/₄ shot triple sec
- ¹/₄ shot crème de menthe (white)

Chill.

SLIPPERY DICK

- ²/₅ shot crème de banana
- ³/₅ shot Irish cream

Chill.

SLIPPERY NIPPLE

- ²/₅ shot peppermint schnapps
- ²/₅ shot Irish cream
- ¹/₅ shot grenadine

Serve.

SNAKEBITE

- 1 shot Yukon Jack
- Dash of lime juice

Serve.

SNOWSHOE

- ³/₅ shot Wild Turkey whiskey
- ²/₅ shot peppermint schnapps

Chill.

S.O.B.

- ⅓ shot brandy
- ⅓ shot Cointreau
- ⅓ shot 151-proof rum

Serve.

STARS AND STRIPES

- ⅓ shot grenadine
- ⅓ shot cream
- ⅓ shot blue curaçao

Layer.

STORM TROOPER

- ½ shot Jägermeister
- ½ shot peppermint schnapps

Chill.

STRAWBERRY SHORTCAKE SHOT

- ⅖ shot strawberry liqueur
- ⅖ shot vodka
- ⅕ shot cream

Chill.

SWEET TART SHOT

- ⅖ shot melon liqueur (Midori)
- ⅖ shot Southern Comfort
- ⅕ shot sour mix

Chill.

TEQUILA SHOT

- 1 shot tequila
- Pinch of salt
- Lime wedge

Lick the salt, drink the shot, suck the lime.

TERMINATOR

- ⅕ shot coffee-flavored liqueur (Kahlúa)
- ⅕ shot Irish cream
- ⅕ shot sambuca

- ⅕ shot Grand Marnier
- ⅕ shot vodka

Layer.

THREE WISE MEN

- ⅓ shot Jack Daniel's
- ⅓ shot Jim Beam
- ⅓ shot Johnnie Walker Red

Serve.

TOOTSIE SHOT

- ½ shot coffee-flavored liqueur (Kahlúa)
- ½ shot orange juice

Chill.

TO THE MOON

- ¼ shot amaretto
- ¼ shot Irish cream
- ¼ shot coffee-flavored liqueur (Kahlúa)
- ¼ shot 151-proof rum

Chill.

TRIPLE T

- ⅓ shot Tanqueray gin
- ⅓ shot tequila
- ⅓ shot Wild Turkey whiskey

Chill.

VAMPIRE

- ⅓ shot vodka
- ⅓ shot Chambord
- ⅓ shot cranberry juice

Chill.

VULCAN MIND PROBE

- ⅓ shot Irish cream
- ⅓ shot peppermint schnapps
- ⅓ shot 151-proof rum
- Large drinking straw

Layer. Suck drink down through straw in one gulp.

WATERMELON

- ⅓ shot vodka
- ⅓ shot strawberry liqueur
- ⅓ shot orange juice

Chill.

WHITE CLOUDS

- ¾ shot sambuca
- ¼ shot soda water

To achieve cloudy look, sambuca must be chilled.

WINDEX

- ½ shot vodka
- ½ shot blue curaçao

Serve.

WOO WOO

- ⅓ shot vodka
- ⅓ shot peach schnapps
- ⅓ shot cranberry juice

Chill.

MORE FUN MIXED DRINKS

AMARETTO AND CREAM
- 1 shot amaretto
- 1½ ounces cream

Shake.

AMARETTO ROSE
- 1 shot amaretto
- Splash of Rose's lime juice
- Soda water

Serve.

ANGEL'S DELIGHT
- ¼ shot grenadine
- ¼ shot triple sec
- ¼ shot sloe gin
- ¼ shot cream

Layer.

ANGEL'S KISS
- ¼ shot crème de cacao (white)
- ¼ shot sloe gin
- ¼ shot brandy
- ¼ shot cream

Layer.

APPLE PIE

- 1½ shots apple schnapps
- Splash of cinnamon schnapps
- Sprinkle of ground cinnamon
- Apple slice

Serve.

B&B

- ½ shot Bénédictine
- ½ shot brandy

Layer.

BACARDI

- 1 shot Bacardi rum
- Splash of lime juice
- Splash of grenadine

Shake.

BANANA BALM

- 1 shot vodka
- ¼ shot crème de banana
- Dash of lime juice
- Soda water

Shake first 3 ingredients, then add soda water.

BANSHEE

- ¾ shot crème de banana
- ¾ shot crème de cacao (white)
- Splash of cream

Shake.

BARBARY COAST

- ½ shot gin
- ½ shot rum
- ½ shot Scotch whisky
- ½ shot crème de cacao (white)
- Splash of cream

Shake.

BEACHCOMBER

- ¾ shot rum
- ¼ shot triple sec
- Splash of lime juice
- Cherry

Moisten rim of glass with lime and dip in sugar. Shake and garnish.

BELMONT STAKES

- ½ shot vodka
- ¼ shot rum
- ¼ shot strawberry liqueur
- Splash of lime juice
- Dash of grenadine
- Orange slice

Shake. For frozen drink, blend with ice. Garnish.

BLACK AND TAN
(HALF AND HALF)

Equal parts of each.

- Ale
- Stout or porter

Layer over ale using inverted spoon as explained in section on "Layering." This drink is usually comprised of Guinness (black) and Harp (tan).

BLACK HAWK

- ¾ shot blended whiskey
- ¾ shot sloe gin
- Cherry

Stir and garnish.

BLACK MAGIC

- 1 shot vodka
- ½ shot coffee-flavored liqueur (Kahlúa)
- Dash of lemon juice
- Twist of lemon

Garnish and serve.

BLOODY MARIA

- 1 shot tequila
- Tomato juice
- Splash of lemon juice
- Dash of Worcestershire sauce
- Dash of Tabasco sauce
- Sprinkle of Celery salt or pepper
- Celery stalk or lime wedge

Garnish and serve.

BLUE LAGOON

- ½ shot vodka
- ½ shot blue curaçao
- Lemonade
- Cherry

Garnish and serve.

BLUE MOON

- 1 shot gin
- ½ shot blue curaçao
- Lemon twist

Shake and garnish.

BLUE SHARK

- ¾ shot vodka
- ¾ shot tequila
- Splash of blue curaçao

Shake.

BOBBY BURNS

- ½ shot Scotch whisky
- ½ shot sweet vermouth
- Dash of Bénédictine
- Twist of lemon

Stir and garnish.

BOCCIE BALL

- 1 shot amaretto
- Orange juice
- Soda water
- Orange slice

Garnish and serve.

BOSTON GOLD

- 1 shot vodka
- Splash of crème de banana
- Orange juice

Stir.

BRANDY COLLINS

- 1 shot brandy
- Sour mix
- Splash of soda water
- Cherry and orange slice

Shake brandy and sour mix, then add soda water. Garnish.

BULLFROG

- 1 shot vodka
- Lemonade
- Lime wedge

Garnish and serve.

CAPRI

- ¾ shot crème de cacao (white)
- ¾ shot crème de banana
- Splash of cream

Shake.

CARA SPOSA

- ¾ shot coffee-flavored brandy
- ¾ shot triple sec
- Splash of cream

Shake.

CARIBBEAN CHAMPAGNE

- 6 ounces champagne (chilled)
- Splash of rum
- Splash of crème de banana

Serve.

CARROL COCKTAIL

- 1 shot brandy
- ½ shot sweet vermouth
- Cherry

Stir and garnish.

CASABLANCA

- 1 shot rum
- Dash of triple sec
- Dash of cherry liqueur (Maraschino)
- Dash of lime juice

Shake.

CHAPEL HILL

- 1 shot bourbon whiskey
- ½ shot triple sec
- Dash of lemon juice
- Orange twist

Shake and garnish.

CHERRY BOMB

- ½ shot vodka
- ½ shot rum
- ½ shot tequila
- Pineapple juice
- Coconut milk
- Splash of milk
- Dash of grenadine

Shake.

CHERRY COLA

- 1 shot dark rum
- ½ shot cherry brandy
- Cola

Serve.

CHIQUITA COCKTAIL

- ¾ shot crème de banana
- ¾ shot Cointreau
- Splash of cream

Shake.

CHOCOLATE RUM

- 1 shot rum
- Dash of 151-proof rum
- Dash of crème de cacao (white)
- Dash of crème de menthe (white)
- Dash of cream

Shake.

CLIMAX

- ¼ shot crème de cacao (white)
- ¼ shot amaretto
- ¼ shot triple sec
- ¼ shot vodka
- ¼ shot crème de banana
- 1 ounce cream

Shake.

CREAMSICLE

- 1 shot amaretto
- Orange juice
- Milk or cream

Shake.

CREAM SODA

- 1 shot amaretto
- Soda water

Serve.

CRICKET

- ¾ shot crème de cacao (white)
- ¾ shot crème de menthe (green)
- Dash of brandy
- 1 ounce cream

Shake.

CRUISE CONTROL

- ½ shot rum
- ¼ shot apricot brandy
- ¼ shot Cointreau
- Splash of lemon juice
- Soda water

Shake.

DAMN-THE-WEATHER

- 1 shot gin
- ½ shot sweet vermouth
- Splash of triple sec
- Splash of orange juice

Shake.

DIRTY MOTHER

- 1 shot brandy
- ½ shot coffee-flavored liqueur (Kahlúa)

Stir.

DREAM

- 1 shot brandy
- ½ shot triple sec
- Dash of anisette

Shake.

EGGNOG FOR ONE

- 1 egg
- 1 teaspoon/packet sugar
- 1 shot desired liquor: brandy, rum, whiskey, or a combination
- 6 ounces milk

- Dusting of grated nutmeg

Beat egg and sugar, then shake entire mix with ice and pour into empty highball glass (no ice).

ELECTRIC LEMONADE

- ¼ shot vodka
- ¼ shot gin
- ¼ shot rum
- ¼ shot tequila
- Splash of triple sec
- Sour mix
- Lemon-lime soda

Shake first 6 ingredients with ice, then add lemon-lime soda.

EL SALVADOR COCKTAIL

- 1 shot rum
- ½ shot hazelnut liqueur (Frangelico)
- Splash of lime juice
- Dash of grenadine

Shake.

FIFTY-FIFTY

- ¾ shot gin
- ¾ shot dry vermouth

Stir.

FLYING DUTCHMAN

- 1½ shots gin
- Dash of triple sec

Shake.

FOXY LADY

- ¾ shot amaretto
- ¾ shot crème de cacao (dark)
- 1½ ounces cream

Shake.

FREE SILVER

- ¾ shot gin
- ¼ shot dark rum
- Dash of cream
- Sour mix
- Soda water

Shake first 4 ingredients, then add soda water.

FROSTBITE

- 1 shot tequila
- ¼ shot crème de cacao (white)
- Splash of blue curaçao
- 2 ounces cream

Shake. For frozen drink, blend with ice.

GENOA COCKTAIL

- 1 shot vodka
- ½ shot Campari
- Orange juice

Shake.

GIN CASSIS

- 1 shot gin
- ¼ shot crème de cassis
- Splash of lemon juice

Shake.

GIN FIZZ

- 1 shot gin
- Sour mix
- Splash of soda water

Shake gin and sour mix with ice, then add soda water.

GIN RICKEY

- 1 shot gin
- Soda water
- Splash of lime juice

Stir.

GLOOM CHASER

- ¾ shot Grand Marnier
- ¾ shot curaçao
- Splash of lemon juice
- Dash of grenadine

Shake.

GODCHILD

- ½ shot vodka
- ½ shot amaretto
- Splash of cream

Shake and strain into champagne glass.

GODFATHER

- 1 shot Scotch whisky
- ½ shot amaretto

Stir.

GODMOTHER

- 1 shot vodka
- ½ shot coffee-flavored liqueur (Kahlúa)

Stir.

GOLDEN DREAM

- 1 shot Galliano
- ¼ shot triple sec
- Splash of orange juice
- Splash of cream

Shake.

GORILLA PUNCH

- ³/₄ shot vodka
- ¹/₄ shot blue curaçao
- Orange juice
- Pineapple juice
- Cherry

Shake and garnish.

GRAND HOTEL

- ³/₄ shot Grand Marnier
- ³/₄ shot gin
- Splash of dry vermouth
- Dash of lemon juice
- Lemon twist

Shake and garnish.

GRAND OCCASION COCKTAIL

- 1 shot rum
- ¹/₄ shot Grand Marnier
- ¹/₄ shot crème de cacao (white)
- Dash of lemon juice

Shake.

GREENBACK

- 1 shot gin
- ¹/₂ shot crème de menthe (green)
- 1 ounce lemon juice

Shake.

GREEN CHARTREUSE NECTAR

- ³/₄ shot apricot schnapps
- ¹/₂ shot Chartreuse (green)

Serve.

GREEN DRAGON

- 1 shot Stolichnaya (Russian vodka)
- ¹/₂ shot Chartreuse (green)

Shake.

GROUND ZERO

- ¹/₂ shot bourbon whiskey
- ¹/₂ shot peppermint schnapps
- ¹/₂ shot vodka
- ¹/₄ shot coffee-flavored liqueur (Kahlúa)

Shake.

HAIRY NAVEL

- ¹/₂ shot peach schnapps
- ¹/₂ shot vodka
- Orange juice

Serve.

HALLEY'S COMFORT

- ¹/₂ shot peach schnapps
- ¹/₂ shot Southern Comfort
- Soda water

Serve.

HAMMERHEAD

- ¹/₂ shot amaretto
- ¹/₂ shot curaçao
- ¹/₂ shot rum
- Dash of Southern Comfort

Shake.

HAWAII SEVEN-O

- 1 shot blended whiskey
- ¹/₂ shot amaretto
- Orange juice
- Splash of piña colada mix

Shake. For frozen drink, blend with ice.

HIGH ROLLER

- 1 shot vodka
- ¹/₂ shot Grand Marnier
- Orange juice
- Dash of grenadine

Shake.

HOMECOMING

- ¾ shot amaretto
- ¾ shot Irish cream

Shake.

HOP TOAD

- ½ shot apricot brandy
- ½ shot rum
- Splash of lime juice

Stir.

ICE PICK

- 1 shot vodka
- Iced tea
- Lemon slice

Garnish and serve.

IGUANA

- ½ shot vodka
- ½ shot tequila
- Dash of coffee-flavored liqueur (Kahlúa)
- 2 ounces sour mix

Shake.

INCIDER

- 1 shot blended whiskey
- Apple cider

Serve.

IRISH RICKEY

- 1 shot Irish whiskey
- Soda water
- Splash of lime juice

Stir.

IRISH SHILLELAGH

- 1 shot Irish whiskey
- Splash of sloe gin

- Splash of rum
- Sour mix
- Raspberries, strawberries, peaches, and a cherry

Shake and garnish.

IXTAPA

- 1 shot coffee-flavored liqueur (Kahlúa)
- ½ shot tequila

Stir.

JADE

- 1 shot rum
- Dash of crème de menthe (green)
- Dash of triple sec
- Dash of lime juice
- 1 teaspoon/packet sugar

Shake.

JAMAICAN CREAM

- ¾ shot Myers's dark rum
- ¾ shot triple sec
- Cream

Serve.

JAMAICAN WIND

- 1 shot Myers's dark rum
- ½ shot coffee-flavored liqueur (Kahlúa)
- Cream

Serve.

JOHN COLLINS

- 1 shot blended whiskey
- Sour mix
- Splash of soda water
- Cherry and orange slice

Shake whiskey and sour mix with ice, then add soda water. Garnish.

JUNGLE JIM

- ¾ shot vodka
- ¾ shot crème de banana
- 1 ounce cream or milk

Shake.

KAHLÚA AND CREAM

- 1½ shots coffee-flavored liqueur (Kahlúa)
- Cream

Stir.

KENTUCKY COCKTAIL

- 1½ shots bourbon whiskey
- 1 ounce pineapple juice

Shake.

KENTUCKY ORANGE BLOSSOM

- 1 shot bourbon whiskey
- Splash of triple sec
- Orange juice

Serve.

KIR ROYALE

- 6 ounces champagne (chilled)
- Splash of crème de cassis

Serve.

KNOCKOUT

- ½ shot apricot brandy
- ½ shot sloe gin
- ½ shot Southern Comfort
- Orange juice

Stir.

KONA COOLER

- 1 shot blended whiskey
- ¼ shot curaçao
- Splash of sweet vermouth
- Splash of lime juice

Serve.

LEPRECHAUN

- 1½ shots Irish whiskey
- Tonic water

Serve.

LIMBO

- 1 shot rum
- ½ shot crème de banana
- 1 ounce orange juice

Shake.

LIME RICKEY

- 1 shot gin
- Splash of lime juice
- Soda water
- Lime wedge

Garnish and serve.

LONG BEACH ICED TEA

- ¼ shot vodka
- ¼ shot gin
- ¼ shot rum
- ¼ shot tequila
- Splash of triple sec
- Sour mix
- Cranberry juice
- Lemon slice

Garnish and serve.

MALIBU WAVE

- ¾ shot tequila
- ¼ shot triple sec
- Dash of blue curaçao
- 1½ ounces sour mix

Shake.

MAMIE GILROY

- 1 shot Scotch whisky
- Ginger ale
- Splash of lime juice

Serve.

MANDEVILLE

- 1 shot rum
- ½ shot dark rum
- Dash of anisette
- Dash of lemon juice
- Dash of grenadine
- Dash of cola

Shake first 5 ingredients, then add cola.

MARMALADE

- 1 shot curaçao
- Tonic water
- Orange slice

Garnish and serve.

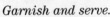

MATADOR

- 1 shot tequila
- 2 ounces pineapple juice
- Splash of lime juice

Shake.

MELON BALL SUNRISE

- ³/₄ shot vodka
- ¹/₄ shot melon liqueur (Midori)
- Orange juice
- Dash of grenadine

Serve.

MIDNIGHT SUN

- 1¹/₂ shots vodka
- Splash of grenadine

Stir.

MIMOSA

- 3 ounces champagne (chilled)
- 3 ounces orange juice

Serve.

MINT JULEP

The Mint Julep is the traditional drink of the Kentucky Derby.

- 4 muddled (crushed) mint leaves
- 2 shots bourbon whiskey
- Dash of water
- 1 teaspoon/packet sugar
- Mint sprig

Stir and garnish.

MOCHA MINT

- ³/₄ shot coffee-flavored liqueur (Kahlúa)
- ³/₄ shot crème de cacao (white)
- ³/₄ shot crème de menthe (white)

Shake.

MONKEY WRENCH

- 1 shot rum
- Grapefruit juice

Stir.

MOSCOW MULE

- 1 shot vodka
- ¾ ounce lime juice
- Ginger ale

Serve.

MOULIN ROUGE

- 1 shot sloe gin
- ½ shot sweet vermouth
- Dash of bitters

Stir.

MUDSLIDE

- ¾ shot vodka
- ¾ shot coffee-flavored liqueur (Kahlúa)
- ¾ shot Irish cream

Shake.

NEGRONI

Ask patron whether drink to be made with sweet or dry vermouth.

- ¾ shot gin
- ¾ shot Campari
- ¾ ounce vermouth (sweet or dry)
- Splash of soda water

Stir.

NINJA TURTLE

- 1 shot gin
- ½ shot blue curaçao
- Orange juice

Stir.

NOCTURNAL

- 1 shot bourbon whiskey
- ½ shot crème de cacao (dark)
- Splash of cream

Shake.

NUTTY STINGER

- 1 shot amaretto
- ½ shot crème de menthe (white)

Shake.

OLYMPIC

- ½ shot brandy
- ½ shot curaçao
- ¾ ounce orange juice

Shake.

ORANGE BLOSSOM

- 1 shot gin
- Orange juice

Serve.

PADDY COCKTAIL

- 1 shot Irish whiskey
- ¾ shot sweet vermouth
- Dash of bitters

Stir.

PAISLEY MARTINI

- 1 shot gin
- Dash of dry vermouth
- Dash of Scotch whisky
- Lemon twist

Stir and garnish.

PANAMA

- ¾ shot dark rum
- ¼ shot crème de cacao (white)
- Cream

Shake.

PAVAROTTI

- 1 shot amaretto
- ¼ shot brandy
- ¼ shot crème de cacao (white)

Shake.

PEPPERMINT PATTY

- ¾ shot crème de cacao (dark)
- ¾ shot crème de menthe (white)
- Cream

Stir.

PERFECT ROB ROY

- 1 shot Scotch whisky
- Dash of sweet vermouth
- Dash of dry vermouth
- Cherry

Stir and garnish.

PINK CREOLE

- 1 shot rum
- Splash of lime juice
- Dash of grenadine
- Dash of cream
- Cherry

Shake and garnish.

PINK LADY

- 1 shot gin
- Splash of grenadine
- 1½ ounces cream

Shake.

PINK LEMONADE

- 1 shot vodka
- Sour mix
- Splash of cranberry juice
- Lemon-lime soda

- Lemon slice

Shake first 3 ingredients, add lemon-lime soda, then garnish.

PINK SQUIRREL

- ½ shot crème de cacao (white)
- ½ shot crème de noyau
- 1 ounce cream

Shake.

PLANTER'S PUNCH

- ¾ shot Myers's dark rum
- ¾ shot rum
- Splash of lime juice
- 1 teaspoon/packet sugar
- Dash of grenadine
- Soda water
- Cherry and orange slice

Shake first 5 ingredients, then add soda water. Garnish.

POPSICLE

- 1 shot amaretto
- Orange juice
- Cream

Stir.

POUSSE-CAFÉ

- ⅕ shot grenadine
- ⅕ shot Chartreuse (yellow)
- ⅕ shot crème de cassis
- ⅕ shot crème de menthe (white)
- ⅕ shot Chartreuse (green)

Layer.

PRESBYTERIAN

- 1 shot whiskey
- Ginger ale
- Soda water

Serve.

PURPLE PASSION

- 1 shot vodka
- Grapefruit juice
- Grape juice

Serve.

QUICKY

- ¾ shot bourbon whiskey
- ¾ shot rum
- Dash of triple sec

Stir.

RAMOS FIZZ

- 1 shot gin
- 1½ ounces sour mix
- Splash of orange juice
- Splash of cream
- 1 egg white
- Soda water

Shake first 5 ingredients, then add soda water.

RASPBERRY SMASH

- ¾ shot vodka
- ¼ shot Chambord
- Pineapple juice

Shake.

RECEPTACLE

- 1 shot vodka
- Splash of cranberry juice
- Splash of orange juice
- Splash of pineapple juice
- Lemon-lime soda
- Cherry and orange slices

Garnish and serve.

RED DEVIL

- ¼ shot vodka
- ¼ shot sloe gin
- ¼ shot Southern Comfort
- ¼ shot triple sec
- ¼ shot crème de banana
- Orange juice
- Dash of lime juice

Shake.

RED LION

- ¾ shot gin
- ¾ shot Grand Marnier
- Splash of orange juice
- Splash of lemon juice

Shake.

RED RUSSIAN

- ¾ shot strawberry liqueur
- ¾ shot vodka
- Cream

Shake.

RICKEY

- 1 shot desired liquor
- Soda water
- Lime wedge.

Garnish and serve.

RITZ FIZZ

- 6 ounces champagne (chilled)
- Dash of amaretto
- Dash of blue curaçao
- Dash of lemon juice
- Lemon twist

Stir and garnish.

ROMAN STINGER

- 1 shot brandy
- ½ shot sambuca
- ½ shot crème de menthe (white)

Shake.

ROSE HALL

- 1 shot dark rum
- ½ shot crème de banana
- 1 ounce orange juice
- Dash of lime juice
- Lime wedge

Shake and garnish.

ROYAL GIN FIZZ

- 1 shot gin
- ½ shot Grand Marnier
- 1 egg white
- Sour mix
- Soda water

Shake first 4 ingredients, then add soda water.

ROYAL SCREW

- 1 shot cognac (brandy)
- 2 ounces orange juice
- Champagne (chilled)

Stir.

RUM RUNNER

- 1 shot gin
- Pineapple juice
- Splash of lime juice
- 1 teaspoon/packet sugar
- Dash of bitters

Shake.

RUPTURED DUCK

- ¾ shot crème de banana
- ¾ shot crème de noyau
- 1 ounce cream

Shake.

RUSSIAN

- ¾ shot gin
- ¾ shot vodka
- ¾ shot crème de cacao (white)

Shake.

RUSSIAN BANANA

- ½ shot vodka
- ½ shot crème de banana
- ½ shot crème de cacao (dark)
- 1 ounce cream

Shake.

ST. PAT'S

- ½ shot crème de menthe (green)
- ½ shot Chartreuse (green)
- ½ shot Irish whiskey

Serve.

SAVE THE PLANET

- ¾ shot melon liqueur (Midori)
- ¾ shot vodka
- Splash of blue curaçao
- Dash of Chartreuse (green)

Shake.

SAXON

- 1½ shots rum
- Splash of lime juice
- Dash of grenadine
- Orange twist

Shake and garnish.

SCARLETT O'HARA

- 1 shot Southern Comfort
- Cranberry juice

Serve.

SCOOTER

- ¾ shot amaretto
- ¾ shot brandy
- 1 ounce cream

Shake.

SEVENTH HEAVEN

- ¾ shot Seagram's 7 whiskey
- ¼ shot amaretto
- Orange juice

Stir.

SHADY LADY

- ¾ shot tequila
- ¾ shot melon liqueur (Midori)
- Grapefruit juice
- Lime wedge and cherry slice

Garnish and serve.

SICILIAN KISS

- 1 shot Southern Comfort
- ½ shot amaretto

Stir.

SIDECAR

- 1 shot brandy
- ½ shot triple sec
- Splash of sour mix

Serve.

SINGAPORE SLING

- 1 shot gin
- ¼ shot cherry brandy
- Sour mix

- Splash of grenadine
- Soda water
- Cherry and orange slice

Shake first 4 ingredients, then add soda water. Garnish.

SIR WALTER RALEIGH

- 1 shot brandy
- ½ shot rum
- Dash of curaçao
- Dash of lime juice
- Dash of grenadine

Shake.

SLEDGEHAMMER

- ½ shot brandy
- ½ shot rum
- ½ shot apple brandy
- Dash of Pernod

Shake.

STONE SOUR

- 1 shot bourbon whiskey
- Dash of crème de menthe (white)
- Splash of lemon juice
- 1 teaspoon/packet sugar
- Soda water

Stir.

STONEWALL

- 1 shot dark rum
- Apple cider

Shake.

SWAMP WATER

- 1 shot rum
- ½ shot blue curaçao
- Orange juice
- Splash of lemon juice

Shake.

T.N.T.

- 1 shot tequila
- Tonic water
- Lime wedge

Garnish and serve.

TENNESSEE

- 1¼ shot rye whiskey
- ¼ shot Maraschino liqueur
- Splash of lemon juice

Shake.

TEQUINI

- 1½ shots tequila
- Dash of dry vermouth
- Lemon twist

Stir and garnish.

TIPPERARY

- ¾ shot Irish whiskey
- ¾ shot Chartreuse (green)
- ¾ shot sweet vermouth

Stir.

TOP BANANA

- ¾ shot vodka
- ¾ shot crème de banana
- Orange juice

Serve.

TOREADOR
- 1 shot tequila
- ½ shot crème de cacao (white)
- Splash of cream

Shake.

TRAFFIC LIGHT
- ½ shot crème de menthe (green)
- ½ shot crème de banana
- ½ shot sloe gin

Layer.

TROPICAL COCKTAIL
- ¾ shot crème de cacao (white)
- ¾ shot Maraschino liqueur
- ¾ shot sweet vermouth
- Dash of bitters

Stir.

VELVET HAMMER
- ½ shot crème de cacao (white)
- ½ shot triple sec
- 2 ounces cream

Shake.

VELVET KISS
- ¾ shot gin
- ¼ shot crème de banana
- 1 ounce cream
- Splash of pineapple juice

Shake.

VICTORY
- 1 shot Pernod
- Soda water
- Splash of grenadine

Serve.

VODKA COOLER

- ³/₄ shot vodka
- ¹/₄ shot sweet vermouth
- Lemon-lime soda

Shake vodka and vermouth, then add lemon-lime soda.

VODKA GRAND MARNIER

- 1 shot vodka
- ¹/₄ shot Grand Marnier
- Dash of lime juice
- Orange slice

Shake and garnish.

WARD EIGHT

- 1 shot bourbon whiskey
- Sour mix
- Splash of grenadine
- Cherry

Shake and garnish.

WHIRLAWAY

- 1 shot bourbon whiskey
- ¹/₂ shot curaçao
- Dash of bitters
- Soda water

Serve.

WILL ROGERS

- 1 shot gin
- ¹/₄ shot dry vermouth
- Dash of triple sec
- Dash of orange juice

Shake.

XANTHIA

- ³/₄ shot Chartreuse (yellow)
- ³/₄ shot cherry brandy
- ³/₄ shot gin

Shake.

YELLOWBIRD

- ½ shot vodka
- ½ shot crème de cacao (white)
- ¼ shot Galliano
- Splash of orange juice
- Splash of cream

Shake.

YELLOW PARROT

- ½ shot anisette
- ½ shot apricot brandy
- ½ shot Chartreuse (yellow)

Shake.

ZOMBIE

- 1 shot rum
- 1 shot dark rum
- ¼ shot apricot brandy
- Orange juice
- Pineapple juice
- Splash of 151-proof rum floated on top
- Cherry and pineapple slice

Shake first 5 ingredients, then float 151-proof rum on top. Garnish and serve.

YOUR MIXED DRINKS
AND NOTES

FROZEN DRINKS

Most frozen drinks should be served in stemmed glasses. Not only do frozen drinks look better in these types of glasses, but more importantly, if held by the stem, the drink will stay cold longer. Because stemmed glasses come in many different sizes, make sure the glass you choose is large enough to hold the frozen drink. If it is not, you may have to alter the amount of ingredients you added to the mix. Unless otherwise noted, add approximately a cup of ice for each frozen drink. For a slushier drink, add more.

BANANA DAIQUIRI

- 1 shot rum
- Splash of crème de banana
- Splash of lime juice
- 1 teaspoon/packet sugar
- 1 ripe banana, sliced

Blend with ice.

BANANA SPLIT

- 1 shot crème de banana
- 1/4 shot crème de cacao (white)
- 1/4 shot crème de noyau
- Splash of milk
- Splash of grenadine

Blend with ice.

BAY BOMBER

- ¼ shot vodka
- ¼ shot gin
- ¼ shot rum
- ¼ shot tequila
- ¼ shot triple sec
- 1 ounce orange juice
- 1 ounce pineapple juice
- 1 ounce cranberry juice
- 1 ounce sour mix
- Splash of 151-proof rum floated on top

Blend liquors and juices with ice, then float 151-proof rum.

BLIZZARD

- 1 shot blended whiskey
- 2 ounces cranberry juice
- Dash of lemon juice
- 2 teaspoons/packets sugar

Blend with ice.

COOL OPERATOR

- ¾ shot melon liqueur (Midori)
- ¼ shot vodka
- ¼ shot rum
- Splash of lime juice
- 3 ounces grapefruit juice
- 3 ounces orange juice

Blend with ice.

DERBY DAIQUIRI

- 1 shot rum
- ½ shot Cointreau
- 1 ounce orange juice
- Splash of lime juice

Blend with about 3 ounces of ice.

FROZEN BIKINI

- 1 shot vodka
- ½ shot peach schnapps
- 2 ounces peach nectar
- 2 ounces orange juice
- Splash of lemon juice
- 1 ounce champagne (chilled)

Blend first 5 ingredients with ice, then add champagne.

FROZEN FUZZY

- ¾ shot peach schnapps
- ¼ shot triple sec
- Splash of lime juice
- Splash of grenadine
- 1 ounce lemon-lime soda

Blend with ice.

FROZEN MATADOR

- 1 shot tequila
- 2 ounces pineapple juice
- Splash of lime juice

Blend with ice.

ICEBALL

- 1 shot gin
- ½ shot crème de menthe (white)
- ½ shot sambuca
- Splash of cream

Blend with ice.

ITALIAN BANANA

- ¾ shot amaretto
- ¾ shot crème de banana
- 2 ounces orange juice
- 1 ounce sour mix
- Cherry

Blend with ice and garnish.

JAMAICAN SHAKE

- 1 shot Myers's dark rum
- ½ shot blended whiskey
- 2 ounces milk or cream

Blend with ice.

MARASCHINO CHERRY

- ¾ shot rum
- ¼ shot amaretto
- ¼ shot peach schnapps
- 1 ounce cranberry juice
- 1 ounce pineapple juice
- Splash of grenadine
- Whipped Cream
- Cherry

Blend liquid ingredients with 2 cups of ice.
Top with whipped cream and a cherry.

MELON COLADA

- 1 shot rum
- ¼ shot melon liqueur (Midori)
- 4 ounces pineapple juice and 2 ounces coconut milk, OR 6 ounces piña colada mix
- Splash of cream
- Cherry

Blend with ice and garnish.

NUTTY COLADA

- 1½ shots amaretto
- 3 ounces pineapple juice and 2 ounces coconut milk, OR 5 ounces piña colada mix
- Splash of cream

Blend with ice.

PEACH DAIQUIRI

- 1 shot rum
- Splash of triple sec
- 1 ounce lime juice

---

* 1 teaspoon/packet sugar
* ½ peach, sliced

Blend with ice.

SCORPION

* 1 shot rum
* ¼ shot brandy
* 2 ounces lemon juice
* 3 ounces orange juice
* Orange slice and cherry

Blend with ice and garnish.

SHARK BITE

* 1 shot dark rum
* Orange juice
* Splash of sour mix
* Splash of grenadine

Blend with ice.

SLOE TEQUILA

* ¾ shot tequila
* ¼ shot sloe gin
* Splash of lime juice

Blend with ice.

TIDAL WAVE

* ¾ shot melon liqueur (Midori)
* ¼ shot rum
* 1 ounce orange juice
* 2 ounces piña colada mix
* 2 ounces sour mix
* Cherry

Blend with ice and garnish.

TROPICAL STORM

- 1 shot dark rum
- ½ shot crème de banana
- 3 ounces orange juice
- Dash of grenadine
- ½ ripe banana, sliced
- Orange slice

Blend with ice and garnish.

ICE CREAM DRINKS

BLUE CLOUD

- ³⁄₄ shot amaretto
- ¹⁄₄ shot blue curaçao
- 2 scoops vanilla ice cream
- Whipped cream
- Cherry

Blend first 3 ingredients, then top with whipped cream and cherry.

CARIBBEAN ICE CREAM

- ¹⁄₂ shot coffee-flavored liqueur (Kahlúa)
- ¹⁄₂ shot dark rum
- Splash of milk or cream
- 2 scoops vanilla ice cream

Blend.

CHOCOLATE BLACK RUSSIAN

- 1 shot vodka
- ¹⁄₂ shot coffee-flavored liqueur (Kahlúa)
- 2 scoops chocolate ice cream

Blend.

DREAMSICLE

- 1 shot amaretto
- Splash of milk or cream
- Splash of orange juice
- 2 scoops vanilla ice cream

Blend.

EMERALD ISLE

- ¾ shot Irish whiskey
- ¾ shot crème de menthe (green)
- 2 scoops vanilla ice cream
- Soda water

Blend first 3 ingredients, then add soda water. Stir after adding soda water.

FROZEN CAPPUCCINO

- ½ shot Irish cream
- ¼ shot coffee-flavored liqueur (Kahlúa)
- ¼ shot hazelnut liqueur (Frangelico)
- Splash of cream
- 1 scoop vanilla ice cream

Blend with ½ cup of ice.

INTERNATIONAL CREAM

- ½ shot Irish cream
- ½ shot coffee-flavored liqueur (Kahlúa)
- Splash of Grand Marnier
- 2 scoops vanilla ice cream
- Splash of milk

Blend.

MISSISSIPPI MUD

- ¾ shot Southern Comfort
- ¾ shot coffee-flavored liqueur (Kahlúa)
- 2 scoops vanilla ice cream

Blend.

NUT 'N' CREAM

- ½ shot amaretto
- ½ shot hazelnut liqueur (Frangelico)
- 2 scoops vanilla ice cream
- Splash of milk
- Grated nutmeg

Blend first 4 ingredients, then dust with grated nutmeg.

ADULT ROOT BEER FLOAT

- ½ shot coffee-flavored liqueur (Kahlúa)
- ½ shot Galliano
- 2 scoops vanilla ice cream
- Cola

Blend first 3 ingredients, then add cola. Stir after adding cola.

RUSSIAN ICE

- 1 shot Stolichnaya (Russian vodka)
- ½ shot coffee-flavored liqueur (Kahlúa)
- Splash of cream
- 2 scoops vanilla ice cream

Blend.

STRAWBERRY SHORTCAKE

- ¾ shot crème de noyau
- ¼ shot crème de cacao (white)
- 2 scoops vanilla ice cream
- 6 strawberries
- Whipped cream
- Splash of strawberry liqueur

Blend first 4 ingredients, add whipped cream, and top it off with strawberry liqueur.

YOUR ICE CREAM DRINKS
AND NOTES

HOT DRINKS

Hot drinks can be a real hit, especially after a long day of skiing or on a cold and stormy night. They are relatively easy to make, and because of the popularity of most hot mixers (i.e. hot chocolate, coffee, etc.) these drinks appeal to a wide range of tastes. To insure their enjoyment, there are a few safety tips which should be followed when serving these drinks.

The cups these drinks are served in should be heated under warm water prior to the addition of the hot drink. Also, because of its superior heat conductivity, it's a good idea to place a metal spoon in the glass or cup to prevent the container from cracking when the hot drink is poured. And finally, be aware that hot drinks can heat a metallic mug in a very short period of time, creating the possibility of burns to the lips of an unsuspecting drinker.

ADULT HOT CHOCOLATE
- 1 shot peppermint schnapps
- Hot chocolate
- Whipped cream

Top with whipped cream and serve.

AMARETTO CAFÉ
- 1 shot amaretto
- Hot black coffee
- Whipped cream

Top with whipped cream and serve.

BAILEYS AND COFFEE

- 1 shot Baileys Irish Cream
- Hot black coffee
- Whipped cream

Top with whipped cream and serve.

COMFORTABLE FIRE

- 1 shot Southern Comfort
- Hot apple cider
- Cinnamon stick

Garnish and serve.

COMFORTABLE MOCHA

- 1 shot Southern Comfort
- Hot chocolate
- Hot black coffee

Serve.

FUZZY NUT

- 1 shot peach schnapps
- ¼ shot amaretto
- Hot chocolate
- Whipped cream

Top with whipped cream and serve.

GROG

- 1 shot rum
- 1 teaspoon/packet sugar
- Dash of lime juice
- Boiling water
- Cinnamon stick

Stir.

HOT BUTTERED RUM

- 1½ shots dark rum
- 1 teaspoon/packet sugar
- 1 teaspoon butter

The Perfect Cocktail

- Boiling water
- Grated nutmeg

Stir and dust with nutmeg.

HOT GOLD

- 1 shot amaretto
- Warm orange juice
- Cinnamon stick

Garnish and serve.

HOT NAIL

- 1 shot Scotch whisky
- ½ shot Drambuie
- Dash of lemon juice
- Boiling water
- Lemon slice and cinnamon stick

Garnish and serve.

HOT PEPPERMINT PATTY

- 1 shot peppermint schnapps
- Hot chocolate
- Splash of milk
- Whipped cream

Top with whipped cream and serve.

HOT TODDY

- 1 shot blended whiskey
- 1 teaspoon/packet sugar
- Boiling water
- Grated nutmeg
- Cinnamon stick

Stir first 3 ingredients, dust with nutmeg, and garnish with cinnamon stick.

HOUSE FIRE

- 1 shot amaretto
- Hot apple cider
- Cinnamon stick

Garnish and serve.

JAMAICAN COFFEE

- ¾ shot Tia Maria
- ¾ shot Jamaican rum
- Hot black coffee
- Whipped cream

Top with whipped cream and serve.

KAHLÚA AND COFFEE

- 1 shot coffee-flavored liqueur (Kahlúa)
- Hot black coffee
- Whipped cream

Top with whipped cream and serve.

KAHLÚA AND HOT CHOCOLATE

- 1 shot coffee-flavored liqueur (Kahlúa)
- Hot chocolate
- Whipped cream

Top with whipped cream and serve.

KIOKI COFFEE

- ¾ shot coffee-flavored liqueur (Kahlúa)
- ¼ shot brandy
- Hot black coffee

Serve.

MALIBU CAFÉ

- 1 shot Malibu rum
- Hot black coffee
- Whipped cream

Top with whipped cream and serve.

MARNIER CAFÉ

- 1 shot Grand Marnier
- Hot black coffee
- Whipped cream

Top with whipped cream and serve.

MEXICAN CAFÉ

- ³/₄ shot coffee-flavored liqueur (Kahlúa)
- ¼ shot tequila
- Hot black coffee

Serve.

NUTTY CAFÉ

- ³/₄ shot amaretto
- ¼ shot hazelnut liqueur (Frangelico)
- Hot black coffee
- Whipped cream

Top with whipped cream and serve.

SWEET DREAMS

- 1 shot rum
- 1 teaspoon/packet sugar
- Warm milk
- Grated nutmeg

Dust with nutmeg and serve.

TEA GROG

- ³/₄ shot dark rum
- ³/₄ shot brandy
- 1 teaspoon honey
- Hot tea
- Cinnamon stick

Stir and add cinnamon stick.

TOM AND JERRY

- 1 egg, separated
- 2 teaspoons/2 packets sugar
- Pinch of baking soda
- ³/₄ shot dark rum
- ³/₄ shot brandy
- Hot milk
- Grated nutmeg

Beat egg and yolk separately. Fold together combining with sugar and baking soda in a heatproof mug. Mix in dark rum and brandy. Fill with hot milk. Dust with nutmeg.

YOUR HOT DRINKS
AND NOTES

ALCOHOL-FREE DRINKS

BEACH BLANKET BINGO
- Cranberry juice
- Grape juice
- Splash of soda water

Serve.

BLACK COW
- 2 scoops of vanilla ice cream
- Root beer

Serve.

CAFÉ MOCHA
- Hot black coffee
- Hot chocolate
- Whipped cream

Top with whipped cream and serve.

CRANBERRY COOLER
- 3 ounces cranberry juice
- Splash of lime juice
- Soda water

Serve.

DIRTY WATER
- Root beer
- Orange soda

Stir.

GENTLE SEA BREEZE

- Grapefruit juice
- Cranberry juice
- Lime wedge

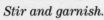

Stir and garnish.

GRAPEBERRY

- Cranberry juice
- Grapefruit juice
- Lime wedge

Garnish and serve.

GREAT GRAPE

- 3 ounces grape juice
- Cranberry juice
- Sour mix
- Lemon-lime soda

Serve.

JUICE COOLER

- Cranberry juice
- Grapefruit juice
- Orange juice
- Pineapple juice
- Ginger ale or soda water

Serve.

JUICER

- Cranberry juice
- Grapefruit juice
- Orange juice
- Pineapple juice

Serve.

LIME COOLER

- Dash of lime juice
- Cola
- Lime wedge

Garnish and serve.

LIMONADE

- 2 ounces sour mix
- Lemon-lime soda
- Soda water
- Lemon slice and lime wedge

Garnish and serve.

NO RUM RICKEY

- 1 ounce lime juice
- Splash of bitters
- Splash of grenadine
- Soda water
- Lime wedge

Garnish and serve.

ORANGE AND TONIC

- Orange juice
- Tonic water
- Orange slice

Garnish and serve.

ORGEAT COCKTAIL

- 1 egg white
- 1 ounce lemon juice
- ¾ ounce orgeat syrup
- Cherry

Shake and garnish.

PAC-MAN

- Ginger ale
- Dash of lemon juice
- Dash of bitters
- Dash of grenadine
- Orange slice and cherry

Garnish and serve.

PLANTER'S JUICE

- Pineapple juice
- Orange juice
- Splash of lime juice

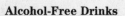

- 1 teaspoon/packet sugar
- Splash of coconut milk
- Splash of grenadine
- Soda water
- Cherry and orange slice

Garnish and serve.

RASP-MA-TAZZ

- 6 ounces pineapple juice
- 1 dozen raspberries (or 6 strawberries, if desired)
- 1 ripe banana

Blend with ice.

ROY ROGERS

- Dash of grenadine
- Cola
- Cherry

Garnish and serve.

SHIRLEY TEMPLE

- Ginger ale
- Dash of grenadine
- Cherry

Garnish and serve.

SOBER DRIVER

- Splash of club soda
- Orange juice

Serve.

SOBER SPRITZER

- 3 ounces white grape juice
- Soda water

Serve.

TEQUILA SUNSET

- Orange juice
- Dash of grenadine

Serve.

The Perfect Cocktail

TOMATO AND TONIC

- 3 ounces tonic water
- Tomato juice
- Lime wedge

Garnish and serve.

TRANSFUSION

- 3 ounces grape juice
- Ginger ale
- Dash of lime juice
- Lime wedge

Garnish and serve.

UNFUZZY NAVEL

- Peach nectar
- Orange juice
- Dash of lemon juice
- Dash of grenadine
- Orange slice

Garnish and serve.

VANILLA COLA

- Splash of vanilla extract (trace amounts of alcohol)
- Cola

Serve.

VIRGIN COLADA

- Pineapple juice
- Coconut milk
- Pineapple slice and cherry

Blend with ice and garnish.

VIRGIN CREAMSICLE

- 2 scoops vanilla ice cream
- 6 ounces orange juice
- Dash of almond extract or orgeat syrup

Blend.

VIRGIN EGGNOG

- 1 egg
- 1 teaspoon/packet sugar
- Dash of vanilla extract (trace amounts of alcohol)
- 1 cup milk
- Grated nutmeg

Beat the egg and sugar, then add the vanilla extract and milk. Pour into empty highball glass (no ice). Dust with nutmeg.

EGGNOGS AND PUNCHES

Eggnog can be made either by using a prepared eggnog mix or by mixing the raw ingredients. The advantage of using a prepared eggnog mix is that salmonella is much less of a threat than when using raw eggs. If you choose to mix the raw ingredients, do so by separating the eggs (yolk from white), and beating the yolk with sugar until it is thick. Then gradually stir in the liquor followed by the milk and cream. In another bowl, beat egg whites until stiff. Keep both mixes refrigerated separately until well-chilled and ready to serve. When ready to serve, carefully fold egg whites in with rest of mix. Be careful not to beat or stir. Never add ice to eggnog. The eggnog recipes below contain approximately ten to twelve servings; increase the ingredients proportionately to yield a greater number of servings.

With a party of twenty or more people punch can be a real crowd-pleaser while saving you both time and money. A punch can be made prior to the party and, once made (as long as you do not run out of it), you can let your guests serve themselves. Depending on the occasion, you can serve a punch in place of a full bar, or at least provide a limited bar when serving punch. Punch and eggnog are especially appropriate around the holidays, but punch can add a special touch to a party at any time during the year.

Because punch will normally be tried by all, young and old, and at times can look so innocent, its strength is something which you must take into account when making. Consider the ages of those at the party and the time of day of the party. If, for example, you were serving a punch for a party in celebration of a graduation from high school, odds are the punch will be consumed by young people, so a weak punch would be advisable.

Punch is relatively easy to make, but there are a few guidelines to follow when making. To cool punch, use one or more large blocks of ice, never ice cubes. Because of the decreased surface area of an ice block, it will dissolve at a much slower rate than ice cubes, therefore keeping the punch colder without diluting it. To make a block of ice, simply fill a large container with water and freeze. You can be creative when making ice blocks by using molds with different designs as is done with Jell-O. Because punch is typically made well before it is served, make sure all carbonated beverages are only added just prior to your guests' arrival, otherwise the punch will go flat. The amount each punch recipe yields is based on 4 ounces per serving.

EGGNOGS

BALTIMORE EGGNOG

- 1 quart prepared eggnog mix; OR 5 eggs
- 16 ounces milk
- 5 ounces cream
- 5 ounces superfine sugar
- 5 ounces brandy
- 5 ounces dark rum
- 5 ounces peach brandy or Madeira wine
- Grated nutmeg

Dust nutmeg over each serving.

BREAKFAST EGGNOG

- 1 quart prepared eggnog mix; OR 5 eggs
- 15 ounces milk
- 5 ounces cream
- 5 ounces superfine sugar
- 10 ounces brandy
- 2 ounces triple sec
- Grated nutmeg

Dust nutmeg over each serving.

EGGNOG (BASIC)

- 1 quart prepared eggnog mix; OR 5 eggs
- 15 ounces milk
- 5 ounces cream
- 5 ounces superfine sugar
- 6 ounces cognac
- 6 ounces dark rum
- Grated nutmeg

Dust nutmeg over each serving.

PUNCHES

BOMBAY PUNCH

- 12 lemons
- Sugar to taste
- One 750-ml. bottle brandy
- One 750-ml. bottle dry sherry
- 4 ounces Maraschino liqueur
- 4 ounces curaçao
- Four 750-ml. bottles champagne
- 2 quarts soda water
- Variety of sliced fruit

Prechill all ingredients. Squeeze lemons into container and mix with enough sugar to sweeten. Pour juice/sugar mix over large block/s of ice in punch bowl and stir in brandy, sherry, Maraschino liqueur, and curaçao. Just prior to serving, gently stir in champagne and soda water. Garnish with fruit slices and serve in punch glasses.

Approximately 60 servings

BRANDY PUNCH

- 12 lemons
- 4 oranges
- Sugar to taste
- 8 ounces curaçao
- Two 750-ml. bottles brandy
- 8 ounces grenadine
- 1 quart soda water, OR one 750-ml. bottle champagne
- Variety of sliced fruit

Prechill all ingredients. Squeeze lemons and oranges into container and mix with enough sugar to sweeten. Pour juice/sugar mix over large block/s of ice in punch bowl. Stir in brandy, curaçao, and grenadine. Just prior to serving, gently stir in either one or a combination of both soda water and champagne. Garnish with fruit slices and serve in punch glasses.

Approximately 35 servings

BUDDHA PUNCH

- One 750-ml. bottle Rhine wine
- 4 ounces curaçao
- 4 ounces rum
- 8 ounces orange juice
- Several dashes of angostura bitters
- 1 quart soda water
- One 750-ml. bottle champagne
- Variety of sliced fruit

Prechill all ingredients. Add all ingredients except soda water and champagne into a punch bowl with block/s of ice. Just prior to serving, gently stir in soda water and

*champagne. Garnish with fruit slices and
serve in punch glasses.*

Approximately 25 servings

CARDINAL PUNCH

- 12 lemons
- Sugar to taste
- Two 750-ml. bottles dry red wine
- 16 ounces brandy
- 16 ounces rum
- 3 ounces sweet vermouth
- 2 quarts soda water
- One 750-ml. bottle champagne
- Variety of sliced fruit

*Prechill all ingredients. Squeeze lemons into
container and mix with enough sugar to
sweeten. Pour juice/sugar mix over large
block/s of ice into punch bowl. Stir in wine,
brandy, rum, and vermouth. Just prior to
serving, gently stir in either one or a
combination of both soda water and chilled
champagne. Garnish with fruit slices and
serve in punch glasses.*

Approximately 50 servings

CHAMPAGNE PUNCH

- 12 lemons
- Sugar to taste
- 16 ounces brandy
- 8 ounces curaçao
- 16 ounces soda water
- Two 750-ml. bottles champagne
- Variety of fruit slices

*Prechill all ingredients. Squeeze lemons into
container and mix with enough sugar to
sweeten. Pour juice/sugar mix over large
block/s of ice into punch bowl. Stir in brandy
and curaçao. Just prior to serving, gently stir
in soda water and champagne. Garnish with
fruit slices and serve in punch glasses.*

Approximately 30 servings

CHAMPAGNE SHERBET PUNCH

- 24 ounces pineapple juice
- 2 ounces lemon juice
- One 750-ml. bottle champagne
- 1 quart lemon, pineapple, or other flavored sherbet

Prechill all ingredients. Stir juices over large block/s of ice. Just prior to serving gently stir in champagne and scoop in sherbet.

Approximately 20 servings

CLARET PUNCH

- 12 lemons
- Sugar to taste
- Two 750-ml. bottles claret
- 16 ounces brandy
- 8 ounces curaçao
- 2 quarts soda water
- Variety of sliced fruit

Prechill all ingredients. Squeeze lemons into container and mix with enough sugar to sweeten. Pour juice/sugar mix over large block/s of ice in punch bowl. Stir in claret, brandy, and curaçao. Just prior to serving, gently stir in soda water. Garnish with fruits of your choice and serve in punch glasses.

Approximately 40 servings

FISH HOUSE PUNCH

- 12 lemons
- Sugar to taste
- One 750-ml. bottle brandy
- 4 ounces peach brandy
- 16 ounces rum
- 2 quarts soda water or flavored soda (cola, 7-Up, or ginger ale)
- Variety of sliced fruit

Prechill all ingredients. Squeeze lemons into container and mix with enough sugar to sweeten. Pour juice/sugar mix over large

---

block/s of ice in punch bowl. Stir in brandies
and rum. Just prior to serving, gently stir in
desired soda. Garnish with fruit slices and
serve in punch glasses.

Approximately 35 servings

SANGRIA

*As with other punches, there are many
variations of Sangria. You may want to
experiment with various ingredients and
combinations of them to arrive at the Sangria
you like best.*

- Two 750-ml. bottles red wine
- 8 ounces rum
- 16 ounces orange juice
- 16 ounces pineapple juice
- 30 ounces canned fruit cocktail
- 1 quart soda water or ginger ale
- Variety of sliced fruit

*Prechill all ingredients. Stir all ingredients
except soda water or ginger ale over large
block/s of ice in punch bowl. Just prior to
serving, gently stir in soda of choice. Garnish
with fruits and serve in red wine glasses.*

Approximately 40 servings

TEQUILA PUNCH

- 1 liter tequila
- Four 750-ml. bottles Sauterne
- 2 quarts various fresh fruit balls and cubes
- One 750-ml. bottle champagne

*Prechill all ingredients. Stir tequila and
Sauterne into a punch bowl over large block/s
of ice. Add various fresh fruit cut into balls
and cubes. Just prior to serving, gently stir in
champagne. Serve in punch cups.*

Approximately 55 servings

WHISKEY PUNCH

- 6 lemons
- Two 750-ml. bottles bourbon or blended whiskey
- 4 ounces curaçao
- 1 quart apple juice
- 2 ounces grenadine
- 4 quarts soda water or ginger ale
- Cherries

Prechill all ingredients. Squeeze lemons into punch bowl over large block/s of ice. Stir in whiskey, curaçao, juice, and grenadine. Just prior to serving, gently stir in soda of choice. Garnish with cherries. Serve in punch glasses.

Approximately 60 servings

WHISKEY SOUR PUNCH

- One 750-ml. bottle bourbon or blended whiskey
- 18 ounces frozen lemonade concentrate (thawed and undiluted)
- 24 ounces orange juice
- 2 quarts soda water
- Orange slices and cherries

Prechill all ingredients. Stir all ingredients except soda water in punch bowl over large block/s of ice. Just prior to serving, gently stir in soda water. Garnish. Serve in punch glasses.

Approximately 35 servings

HOT PUNCHES

BANDIT'S BREW

- 12 ounces dark rum
- 1 quart tea
- 3 tablespoons butter
- 4 ounces sugar
- ½ teaspoon grated nutmeg
- 4 ounces brandy

Heat all ingredients except brandy in a saucepan until mix boils. Heat brandy in separate saucepan until it is warm; add brandy to mix. Serve punch in heatproof glasses.

Approximately 12 servings

GLÜG

- 8 ounces water
- 1 cup raisins
- 15 cardamom seeds
- 3 cinnamon sticks
- 4 cloves
- 2 dry orange peels

Boil the above ingredients for 10 to 15 minutes in saucepan. Add following ingredients to the mix and boil entire mix.

- 4 quarts port wine
- One 750-ml. bottle brandy
- 16 ounces rum
- ½ cup sugar

Let mix boil for around a minute then turn off burner and ignite the mix. Allow the mix to burn for about 15 seconds. Serve hot in punch glasses.

Approximately 50 servings

HOT APPLE BRANDY

- 1½ quarts apple juice
- 3 cinnamon sticks
- ½ teaspoon ground cloves
- 12 ounces apricot brandy

In a saucepan, simmer all ingredients except for apricot brandy over low heat. Add apricot brandy to mix after it has simmered for 15 minutes, and allow to simmer for an additional 15 minutes (total of 30 minutes). Serve warm in brandy snifters.

Approximately 15 servings

HOT APPLE RUM PUNCH

- 1 liter dark rum
- 1 quart apple cider
- 3 broken cinnamon sticks
- 1½ tablespoons butter

Heat all ingredients in saucepan until mix almost boils. Serve punch hot in heatproof glasses.

Approximately 15 servings

ALCOHOL-FREE PUNCHES

JUNGLE JUICE

- One 12-ounce can frozen orange juice concentrate, thawed and undiluted
- One 12-ounce can frozen lemonade concentrate, thawed and undiluted
- One 12-ounce can frozen grape juice concentrate, thawed and undiluted
- 2¼ quarts water
- 1 quart ginger ale
- 1 pint raspberry sherbet

Prechill all ingredients. Stir concentrates and water over large ice block/s in a punch bowl. Just prior to serving, gently stir ginger ale in and spoon sherbet on top of punch. Serve in punch glasses.

Approximately 40 servings

PINEBERRY PUNCH

- 2 quarts pineapple juice
- 2 quarts cranberry juice
- 16 ounces soda water
- 16 ounces ginger ale
- Variety of sliced fruit

Prechill all ingredients. Stir juices over ice block/s in punch bowl. Just prior to serving, gently stir in sodas. Garnish with fruit slices.

Approximately 40 servings

RAINBOW PUNCH

- 8 ounces orange juice
- 8 ounces pineapple juice
- 8 ounces red Hawaiian Punch
- 1 quart soda water
- 1 quart ginger ale
- 1 quart rainbow sherbet

Prechill all ingredients. Stir juices and punch over ice block/s in a punch bowl. Just prior to serving, gently stir in sodas and spoon sherbet on top of punch. Serve in punch glasses.

Approximately 30 servings

VERRY BERRY PUNCH

- 12 raspberries
- 2 quarts cranberry juice
- 24 ounces raspberry soda
- 1 quart raspberry sherbet

Prechill all ingredients. Stir raspberries and cranberry juice over ice block/s in a punch bowl. Just prior to serving, gently stir in raspberry soda and spoon sherbet on top of punch. Serve in punch glasses.

Approximately 30 servings

APPENDIX 1
POINTERS FROM
THE PRO

ICE

Never scoop ice with the glass that you will serve a drink in. Always use an ice scoop or a shaker, never a glass object. There are two reasons for this. First, it looks very unsanitary—patrons may think, correctly or not, that you are filling unclean glasses directly from the ice bin. This impression comes from the fact that patrons often prefer their glasses to be refilled using the old ice rather than receiving their next drink in a clean, empty glass (it is said that alcohol gets concentrated in ice). Second and more importantly, it is very easy to break glass in the ice bin. When this happens, and eventually it will, you *must* empty all the ice from the bin. Then, clean the bin with hot water and a rag, to get all of the broken glass. Then refill the bin with ice. This is a very time-consuming procedure, so get in the habit of using a scoop.

BLEEDING

If a specific beer or wine tap, or the soda gun, has not been used for a few hours its line should be bled. Bleeding a line is simply running the line to clear the beer, wine, or soda which collects there. The liquid that sits in the lines becomes stale after a few hours, and thus needs to be dumped. This is important because stale beer, wine which has become vinegar, or flat soda is not a pleasant drink.

THE CALLING ORDER

A calling order is a system where the waitress orders drinks from the bartender in a specific chronological order. Many bars do not practice a calling order, although it is something all bars should utilize. A calling order limits confusion and speeds the entire ordering process.

For example, a typical calling order might be as follows: 1) mixed drinks; 2) soft drinks; 3) wine; 4) beer; 5) shots. This means that if the order was a glass of red wine, a shot of sambuca, four bottles of Miller Genuine Draft (beer), and two Vodka and Tonics, the waitress would not simply order it in the above miscellaneous fashion, but rather in the proper calling order. For this particular drink order we will use the calling order we have listed above. The waitress should begin the order by saying "ordering," then stating any mixed drinks followed by the number of these drinks—in this case two times—then stating any soft drinks, the number of each, and so on. Stating the number of each drink after the drink is much easier to remember, and though it may not sound so, is much less confusing than stating the number followed by the drink.

Her complete order would sound like this: "ORDERING, vodka tonic two times, Genuine Draft four times, red wine one glass, sambuca one shot." It cannot be stressed enough how much easier a bartender's night can be if a calling order is practiced. It makes the entire process, from remembering what was ordered to calculating the order's total price, much easier.

A great number of the tips a bartender receives are $1 bills. Often, especially on busy nights, the register will run out of these bills. Therefore, instead of stuffing your bills into a jar, as most bartenders do, it is a good idea to either lay them flat, one on top of another, or keep them in a jar or pitcher in an orderly fashion. If and when the register runs out of singles, you are ready with a reserve stack. Don't forget to reimburse your tip jar equitably with larger bills from the same register in which you placed the singles.

There are many tricks for increasing your tips, including laying out a couple of $1 bills on the bar. (This is supposed to catch your patrons' eyes and remind them to tip.) Some bartenders are always ready to light a patron's cigarette, others have their regular customers' drinks waiting for them as they sit down. These may or may not work, but the only guaranteed way to increase your tips (other than simply making good drinks and being polite) is keeping the bar clean. This means emptying ashtrays with one or more cigarette butts. The bar should be wiped down frequently, as liquid, napkins, and cigarette wrappers collect upon it. This also means keeping glasses clean; lipstick and other stains are *very* noticeable on glass if not removed, and will definitely hurt your tips.

SERVING

If there are both women and men in a group, it is proper to serve the women their drinks before the men.

Drinks served to patrons seated at the bar should be accompanied by a napkin or coaster.

If someone asks for a chilled beer glass or liquor glass (most notably the cocktail glass), this can be done even if you have not planned ahead or do not have space in the cooler to chill glasses. Place the glass to be chilled in a bucket or large pitcher with ice, cover the glass with ice, and spin the glass for approximately 20 to 30 seconds. The glass will be properly chilled enough to have condensation on its sides.

Many bars lack ginger ale in the soda gun. This is no problem. Ginger ale can be made very easily if the gun has lemon-lime soda (7-Up or Sprite) and cola. Simply fill the glass almost all the way to the top with lemon-lime soda, then add a little more than a splash of cola. Stir it gently and *voilà:* ginger ale.

When making a drink calling for two primary mixers, both of which are available on the soda gun, push the buttons for both mixers simultaneously. The glass will fill faster and contain exactly half of each of the mixers (for example, Seabreeze, which has cranberry and grapefruit juice as its primary mixers).

If there is enough room in either the cooler or the ice bin, put in bottles of your bar's most popular shots which are served chilled. Doing this will save valuable time which would otherwise be used chilling those shots. It is also smart, and in many bars a necessity, to keep premixed bottles of Watermelon and Kamikaze shots. Due to the fruit juices they contain, these shots are perishable, and the bottles must be kept cold.

IMPROVISING

When you get behind the bar, you will realize that oftentimes you won't have certain tools of the trade, and therefore must improvise. The absence of proper tools may be due to bartenders not replacing them where they belong. If you've been asked to make a chilled drink and you can't find the strainer, simply chill the liquid in either a glass or a shaker and then place an empty glass right side up into the mix. Hold both the glass and the container and begin pouring slowly into the shot or cocktail glass. The empty glass will work as a strainer and hold the ice while allowing the liquid to flow around the edges. In order to be ready for the necessity of using this technique, practice with water before pouring with liquor.

POURING BEER

Many new bartenders have difficulty pouring draft beers, and allow too much head to form on the beer. New bartenders often think a bar keg is just like a party keg, and all one needs to do is tilt the glass while pouring to eliminate the foam. This is not the case, because bar kegs are better refrigerated and are powered by carbon dioxide. The key to pouring beer from a bar tapper is to allow the first squirt from the tapper (usually foam) to miss the glass, then to capture the rest of the beer with the glass touching the metal spout. The glass should be tilted at about 15 degrees, and gradually the angle should increase until the glass is full and upright. The beer should have about a half inch of head.

MISCELLANEOUS

If for any reason it becomes necessary to taste a patron's drink, usually to check its contents, it can be done easily and sanitarily. Simply submerge a straw or mixing rod into the drink, then place your finger over the top of the device; enough liquid will be captured in the straw to taste test. Do not double dip with the same straw!

When pouring a drink from a bottle of liquor which is almost empty, always use a jigger. If the bottle empties perfectly at a shot, the patron, if watching, will feel shortchanged. If it empties at under a shot, your count will be off. Fill the jigger with the contents from two bottles and you won't risk disappointing the customer.

If someone orders a drink, usually a shot, and requests a chaser, the chaser is generally at no charge. The chaser, usually cola, should be served without ice in the small rocks glass.

Whenever someone orders a nonalcoholic beer, always offer the patron a glass. Many people are self-conscious about drinking nonalcoholic beer in a bar.

Because a speed rack is often used without consciously looking at the bottle which is poured, it is a good idea to divide bottles by appearance. For example, split the vodka and gin bottles by placing a whiskey bottle between them. This should be done because vodka and gin look alike and many times you will not have time to look at the label. You will quickly notice the mistake if you grab a dark bottle of whiskey rather than a clear bottle of either gin or vodka.

The practice of stirring a patron's drink has for the most part been phased out. If a bartender is pouring mixers from a soda gun, he or she does not need to stir a patron's drink, even if the mixer is uncarbonated. The pressure of the mixer coming from the soda gun will mix the drink.

It is very important to clean both shaker shells and the strainer after each use. An unclean shaker and strainer will taint future drinks.

If you are out of Seagram's 7 or Jack Daniel's and someone orders a 7&7, or a Jack and Coke, do not reach for a substitute or for bar whiskey to complete the order. Simply by ordering these drinks, the customer is making a "call" order. Suggest a similar brand or tell him or her what brands are stocked. If the patron sees you pouring something other than the brand requested, he or she has a right to complain.

When making any drink calling for the rim to be salted, the rim must be dampened in order for the salt to stick to it. Dampen the rim by taking a lime and rubbing it around the glass's rim. Then take the glass and spin it in the salt. The glass is now ready for the drink.

When opening a bottle of wine with a corkscrew, make sure the corkscrew does not pierce the opposite end of the cork. If the corkscrew pushes through the entire cork, it will break the cork, sending pieces of cork into the wine. This is a pet peeve for many wine drinkers, especially those having to remove small pieces of cork from expensive wine.

If you need crushed or shaved ice yet have no access to an electric ice-crusher, you have two options. You can either use an electric blender or crush the ice by hand. If you decide to use an electric blender you should be aware that, unless you have a very heavy-duty model with a sharp blade, crushing ice in your blender could damage it. Remember when making frozen drinks that you have quite a bit of liquid mix, which will act as a catalyst in the process, thereby taking some strain off of your blender. To crush ice by hand, simply fill a plastic bag with ice and wrap a towel around the bag. Then place the bag and towel on a counter or table and crush the ice either with a rolling pin (by rolling over the bag) or by hitting the bag with a blunt object such as a mallet, hammer, or the barrel end of a bat.

Some people make opening champagne a major job, but if done correctly, it is a simple task. Instead of fighting to twist and pull the champagne cork, hold the cork firmly with one hand while twisting the bottle with the other hand. When removing a cork, always point the bottle away from everyone, including yourself.

APPENDIX 2
BAR
TERMINOLOGY

Call: When a patron specifies the brand of alcohol to be used in his or her drink. For instance, if someone ordered a Tanqueray and Tonic instead of a Gin and Tonic, this would be a *call* drink. Whenever either call or top-shelf liquor is requested, the patron has ordered a call drink. Never use any brand but the brand called; if you are out of that brand, let the patron know what brands in the desired category you do have.

Chaser: Sometimes called a "side" or a "back," this is a mixer which is served in a separate glass and consumed just after a shot. A chaser masks the often harsh taste of the shot. Cola is the most frequently requested chaser.

Collins: A class of drinks including John Collins (whiskey), Rum Collins, Tequila Collins, the ever-famous Tom Collins (gin), and the Vodka Collins. This class of drinks made in the collins glass consists of the specified liquor, sour mix, club soda, and a cherry. The names of the different Collins drinks represent the liquors used in the making.

Comp: Short for complimentary drink. The house or bartender will often "comp" the patron a drink. Most bars have policies on complimentary drinks. Check the policy of your bar.

Dash: This refers to a quantity of liquid. A dash is technically about one-sixth of a teaspoon, or several drops. Those ingredients which often only require a dash (bitters, Tabasco, etc.), have pourers which allow this amount to be dispensed by giving the bottle a quick flip over the drink.

Double: A drink requested with double the amount of liquor that is served in the normal version of that drink. For example, a double Rum and Coke would contain two shots of rum instead of just one.

Dry: This refers to the amount of dry vermouth added to a Martini. The less dry vermouth added to a Martini, the drier it is. An Extra Dry Martini has just a trace of dry vermouth.

Garbage: Any garnish that does not improve the taste of the drink it is placed in. In other words, the purpose of "garbage" is to make the drink look better. Examples of garbage are a celery stalk in a Bloody Mary or a Maraschino cherry in a Manhattan.

Mixer: Any nonalcoholic liquid mixed with alcohol in a drink.

Neat: Any shot of liquor or liqueur which is consumed by itself without ice is "neat." For example, if someone ordered a shot of whiskey neat, he or she would be ordering a shot of whiskey in a shot glass, unchilled.

Perfect: This is a term used with drinks calling for vermouth. Any drink calling for vermouth, either dry or sweet, can be made perfect by adding equal parts of both dry and sweet vermouth. For example, a Perfect Manhattan contains not only sweet vermouth, but an equal portion of dry vermouth.

Proof: Refers to the percent of alcohol in a given beverage. This number is derived from a scale wherein 200 is equal to 100 percent alcohol. Therefore, a bottle containing liquor which is 86 proof is in fact 43 percent alcohol (divide proof by two to arrive at the percent of alcohol). The proof of a beverage is printed on the labels of all liquor bottles.

Short: This term is used in reference to "underpouring" a drink, or pouring less than the required amount of alcohol. It is not an accepted bartending practice. A good rule of thumb is: never short the customer (underpour) or the house (overpour).

Splash: This refers to a quantity of liquid. A splash is a little less than $\frac{1}{2}$ ounce. Those ingredients that often only require a splash (such as lime juice, grenadine, and so on) have pourers allowing this amount to be easily dispensed. You should learn to dispense a splash by simply giving the bottle a quick squirt over the drink.

Tall: A patron will order a "tall" when he or she wants the given drink served in a tall glass. This request is usually made when the drink is normally served in a small rocks glass. A tall is ordered because the patron wants a greater quantity of mixer than can be added to a small rocks glass. Remember, only add more mixer in a tall; the amount of liquor stays the same.

Twist: A "twist" or a "twist of lemon" is a piece of lemon peel. A twist should be a rectangular piece approximately 1 inch by $\frac{1}{4}$ inch. It is called a "twist" because it is twisted above the drink before it is added to the drink. To impart more of the peel's taste to the drink, rub the twist along the rim of the glass. Though the peels of fruits other than the lemon are used to garnish drinks, their use is very infrequent. Often, when patrons order a drink such as Vodka and Tonic with a "twist of lime," they mean a lime wedge; most customers are simply not up on the proper bar lingo.

Virgin: A drink made without liquor. A Virgin Mary is an example of a virgin drink; it contains all the ingredients of a Bloody Mary except the vodka.

APPENDIX 3
BARTENDING
AT HOME

Have you ever wondered why drinks taste so much better at a bar than they do at home or at un-catered parties? In this section we will discuss the difference between drinks made in a bar and drinks made at home so you will be able to make drinks which taste, feel, and look every bit as good as those made by the pros.

The most obvious problem with most drinks made at home is that often incorrect quantities of alcohol and mixers are used. As explained on page 9, a shot is an unregulated amount, usually around an ounce. Because this quantity is arbitrary, and, for the sake of consistency, you should decide what quantity a shot will be at your home bar. This does not mean that if someone else is pouring a drink they must abide by this amount. It is simply an aid for you in making uniform drinks every time, as a cookie cutter is an aid in making a uniform cookie. Establishing a gauge on how much alcohol you are pouring is also helpful if you are asked to alter someone's drink. A guest may request their next drink be either a little "stronger" (more alcohol) or a little "weaker" (less alcohol). If you are using a consistent shot you will know how much alcohol was added to the last drink and can adjust the next drink accordingly. It must also be noted that there is a degree of responsibility when entertaining in one's home. In this day of increased liability, knowing how much alcohol you have poured in each drink will allow you to better gauge who is capable of driving and who is not. When determining the quantity of a shot in your home, the decision should be based on your taste preferences, economic factors (important when throwing a large party) and even the aforementioned legal factors. When you have made this decision you should purchase a jigger (a shot glass can be used as well) which will help in regulating this quantity of liquor. Keep in mind if you would rather not use a jigger, you can also produce a consistent quantity utilizing the free-pouring techniques explained on page 17.

Now that you have regulated the quantity of alcohol, it is time to regulate the quantity of mixers. This is the easy part, but only if you have proper-sized bar glasses. This is important because for all drinks served over ice, the bar glass regulates the amount of primary mixer added to the drink. When you pour the primary mixer, leave only enough room at the top of the glass to avoid spillage, or space enough for secondary mixers. Secondary mixers call for quantities that are easily regulated by the bartender, usually a dash or a splash. For a listing on the size specifications of various bar glasses see page 26. The mixers added to drinks which are served straight up or to any other drink which is not made in its glass cannot be regulated by the bar glass and therefore must be measured or estimated by the bartender, if only by his or her eye. It is usually fairly easy to estimate amounts for drinks served straight up. There is not very much liquid in a drink served "up," and therefore each of its mixers is usually no larger than around an ounce, or about two splashes.

The glasses you choose for your bar are not only an important component for regulating the quantity of mixers added to drinks but also important for the presentation of the drink. Have you ever gone to someone's home and they served you a Vodka and

Tonic in a huge convenience-store cup or in a beer mug? The drink does not feel the same. The appearance and feel of the glass are very important for the drink. The ingredients may be identical, but the perception is that the drink served in the proper glass is a better drink.

So now you have the proper quantities of ingredients in the correct glass. Is it ready to be served? If you were at home the answer might be yes; however, if you were at a bar the answer is a definite no. The reason is that the drink is unfinished. If a bartender forgot to add the lime to your Vodka and Tonic, you would likely recognize that the drink was served incomplete. To get the most out of your drinks at home, go the extra step and add the garnish and the straw or mixing rod. The garnish will improve the drink's flavor and augment its appearance, while the straw or mixing rod will lend its usefulness to the drink and give the drink the same legitimacy it would have if served in a bar.

STOCKING THE HOME BAR

The Perfect Cocktail divides the home bar into three different divisions, the Basic Bar, the Solid Bar, and the Complete Bar. The ingredients in the Basic Bar should adequately fulfill the basic drinking preferences of most people, but will not allow for much creativity in the drinks which can be made. The Solid Bar includes all those components listed in the Basic Bar as well as ingredients not found there, making it a step above the Basic Bar. The Solid Bar level should fulfill the drinking preferences of most people and will allow for the creation of a generous variety of mixed drinks and mixed shots. The Complete Bar includes all those components listed in both the Basic Bar and the Solid Bar sections. A bar containing this variety of contents has roughly the same stock as that of a neighborhood bar. But as with anything, quality is more important than quantity. Therefore, when purchasing for your home bar you should base your purchasing decision not simply on price but on your personal tastes and the advice of others, including those in the liquor business (i.e., bartenders, liquor store employees, etc.). Remember, although the untrained taste buds may not be able to taste the difference between a cheap or an expensive vodka in a Screwdriver, there is nothing worse than the hangover from cheap liquor.

LIQUOR

When stocking your home bar, there are several things to keep in mind, the most important of which is who you will be entertaining. If you plan to have a small group, this will limit the amount of liquor which you will need to purchase. On the other hand, if you have large parties, chances are those you will entertain will have a wide range of taste preferences and consequently you should purchase a greater quantity and diversity of liquors. Liquor is the most important component of the bar, as well as the most expensive. It should be noted that the lists below take into account established norms, not your own or your friends' drinking preferences. Therefore, you should feel free to revise these lists in order to accommodate yourself and those you entertain.

THE BASIC BAR

Vodka

Blended whiskey/bourbon

Rum (light)

THE SOLID BAR

Gin

Scotch whisky

Brandy/cognac

THE COMPLETE BAR

Canadian whisky

Irish whiskey

Rum (dark)

LIQUEUR

Although liqueur is not used as much as liquor in mixed drinks, it is more popular than liquor in mixed shots. Liqueurs are also popular as after-dinner drinks, and in frappés (over shaved ice) or straight up. The following lists include the most popular liqueurs, but there are many more than what is here.

THE BASIC BAR

Triple sec

Coffee-flavored liqueur (Kahlúa*)

Amaretto

Dry vermouth

Sweet vermouth

THE SOLID BAR

Grand Marnier*

Irish cream

Crème de cassis

Sloe gin

Jägermeister*

Southern Comfort*

Crème de menthe

Sambuca

Peppermint or other flavored schnapps

THE COMPLETE BAR

Melon liqueur (Midori*)

Crème de cacao

Curaçao

Drambuie*

Hazelnut liqueur (Frangelico*)

Galliano*

Crème de banana

Ouzo

Tia Maria*

Yukon Jack*

Anisette

Bénédictine*

Campari*

*Denotes those liqueurs which are proprietary (brand-name).

When purchasing wine for your home bar you should, as with other components of the home bar, base your decisions on the popularity of individual wines among you and those you entertain. If you rarely serve wine, a small selection of white and red wines should be sufficient. If you and those you entertain enjoy and appreciate wine, you should try to acquire a diverse supply of it. Always store wine in a dark, cool, and dry place. Corked bottles should be stored on their sides to keep the cork moist. If a cork dries and shrinks, oxygen gets into the bottle, prematurely oxidizing the wine. Wine should oxidize (or "breathe") for at least ten to fifteen minutes in the glass before drinking. It will take longer for the wine to breathe in the bottle because the neck of the bottle restricts the flow of air, and the surface area of the wine is decreased when in the bottle as opposed to in a wine glass. If you taste wine just after opening the bottle and then taste the same wine after ten or fifteen minutes, even an untrained palate can notice the improved taste. If you are serving an old bottle of red wine which has been in storage for a few years, a degree of sediment will have collected at the bottom of the bottle; prior to serving, separate the wine from the sediment by pouring the wine slowly and carefully into a decanter, leaving the sediment in the bottle for disposal. A bottle of wine which has been opened but not finished should be stored in a refrigerator with its cork in place. Though opened wine will not keep for more than a few days before turning to vinegar, storing it in a refrigerator will lengthen its life. There are countless varieties of wine. The list below is not a comprehensive list, it simply contains some of the most popular varieties of wine, wines to consider when purchasing for your home bar.

THE BASIC BAR

Chardonnay (white)

Cabernet Sauvignon (red)

THE SOLID BAR

Burgundy (red)

Pinot Noir (red)

Sauvignon Blanc (white)

Chianti (red)

White Zinfandel (white)

THE COMPLETE BAR

Champagne or sparkling wine

Port or sherry (fortified wine)

BEER

Beer can be grouped in much the same way as wine. Having a few different selections of beer should satisfy most of your guests. Your bar should include a major domestic lager, a light beer, and a nonalcoholic beer. The nineties have spawned a micro-brewing trend, therefore a micro-brewed beer or an import behind your bar will satisfy that growing portion of beer drinkers who prefer a thicker, more distinct-tasting beer.

THE BASIC BAR

Lager

Light beer (lager)

Nonalcoholic beer

THE SOLID BAR

Ale

THE COMPLETE BAR

Porter

Stout

MIXERS

Mixers are an inexpensive yet important part of the home bar. They are also difficult to stock, because most are either perishable or will become flat in time after opening. Because milk and juices will not last much more than a week, these perishable mixers should be purchased only when they will be used. Remember, to avoid problems with the freshness of mixers, keep a small stock of mixers and stock up on perishables just prior to parties. Instead of stocking expensive raw ingredients, you may want to purchase more reasonably priced and time-efficient premade mixes, such as piña colada mix, which combines pineapple juice and coconut milk. The most frequently used of all mixers are tonic water, orange juice, and cola.

THE BASIC BAR

Cola

Tonic water

Orange juice

Lemon-lime soda (7-Up)

Sour mix

Lime juice

Water

Grenadine

THE SOLID BAR

Cream

Coffee

Tomato juice

Cranberry juice

Soda water

Lemon juice

Ginger ale

Milk

THE COMPLETE BAR

Pineapple juice

Ice cream

Orgeat syrup

Grapefruit juice

Strawberries or strawberry mix

Coconut milk

Bananas or banana mix

Though condiments are not used in most drinks, they will be missed if absent in those drinks that do call for them. It should also be noted that there are many people who enjoy ingredients not called for in a "normal" recipe; for instance, don't be surprised if someone asks for horseradish in their Bloody Mary.

THE BASIC BAR

Sugar

Coarse salt

Pepper

Tabasco sauce

THE SOLID BAR

Bitters

Whipped cream

Worcestershire sauce

THE COMPLETE BAR

Horseradish

Celery salt

Grated nutmeg

GARNISHES

This part of the home bar is most often neglected. If you want your drinks to taste and look as good as those made in a bar, you should not ignore the garnishes. As with mixers, the freshness of garnishes is important.

THE BASIC BAR

Limes

Lemons

Oranges

THE SOLID BAR

Maraschino cherries

Celery stalks

Stuffed olives

THE COMPLETE BAR

Strawberries

Cinnamon sticks

Pineapple

Cocktail onions

BAR GLASSES

When purchasing bar glasses keep in mind the number of people you plan to entertain. It may be unnecessary to purchase more than a half dozen of any of the glasses below. Rocks glasses are the most often used of all bar glasses. Though it is nice to serve a given drink in its correct glass, rocks glasses are the most versatile of all glasses and if needed can be used to serve most any drink. Depending on your formality and your budget, it may also be within your protocol to purchase only one type of wineglass. If this is the case, the best all-purpose wineglass is the balloon glass. With its wide bowl and tapered rim a balloon glass can amply accommodate both white and red wine. As for the beer glasses, any one of those listed in the Basic Bar section will suffice.

THE BASIC BAR

Large rocks/Highball glass

Small rocks/Old-Fashioned glass

All-purpose wineglass (balloon)

Beer mug or pilsner glass or pint glass

Cocktail/Martini glass

Shot glass

THE SOLID BAR

Brandy snifter

Irish Coffee cup

Red wine glass

White wine glass

THE COMPLETE BAR

Collins glass

Whiskey Sour glass

Champagne flute

Cordial or pony

Margarita glass

BAR EQUIPMENT

Having the right equipment behind the bar will enable the bartender to make better drinks in a more timely manner. The proper bar equipment will also enable the bartender to make a wider variety of drinks.

THE BASIC BAR

Jigger

Can/bottle opener and corkscrew/(bartender's friend)

Shaker set

Ice bucket/cooler

Bar spoon

THE SOLID BAR

Strainer

Paring knife

Ice scoop

THE COMPLETE BAR

Electric blender

Speedpourers (if you free pour)

Other items which, though not essential to the making of drinks, will greatly aid in keeping the bar area clean, are trash cans and ashtrays (if you permit smoking). A bar works best with two trash cans, a wet trash for pouring leftover drinks into and a dry trash for napkins and other nonliquid waste. If you make sure only to pour liquids in the wet trash, it can be dumped frequently into a utility sink, basement toilet, or other large drain.

MISCELLANEOUS

Fresh ice is an extremely important part of any mixed drink. All one needs to do to prove this theory is to add some stale, freezer-burned ice to their next drink. Ice can also be tainted in an odorous freezer. It is important that the ice you use for your home bar is fresh and has no distinct flavor. Ice in the form of cubes is best.

Though not as important as ice, the other items listed below will improve any drink. The minimal cost of these items makes it completely worthwhile to include them when stocking your home bar.

THE BASIC BAR

Ice

THE SOLID BAR

Mixing rods (small straws)
Straws

THE COMPLETE BAR

Cocktail napkins/coasters

APPENDIX 4
PLANNING AND
THROWING A
PARTY

A party is the true testing grounds for your home bar and bartending skills. When planning for a party, you must first purchase the stock for your bar. If you have a good idea of what people will be drinking, you should base your purchases on this knowledge. If you are unsure of what your guests will be drinking, you need to look at several factors which may predict their tastes. Because there are trends in drinking, the most important factor is the age of your guests. Younger guests (thirty-five and under) on the average prefer weaker drinks, beer, wine, and mild mixed drinks. Older drinkers have an inclination toward stronger drinks, often unmixed, such as Scotch on the rocks and brandy straight up. Beer is popular in all age groups.

The season or climate has a lot to do with drink preferences as well. Warm weather seems to encourage lighter drinks, like light beer, white wine, and fruity mixed drinks. As the temperature drops, drinkers move toward heavier beers, red wine, fortified wines, mixed drinks with warm ingredients such as coffee or tea, and dark liquors such as brandy. The time of day at which your party will take place is another factor in determining what drinks will be popular. A late-morning or midday party will see a strong demand for juice and vodka drinks such as the Bloody Mary or the Screwdriver. Some guests will abstain from drinking altogether at this time of day, so you should make sure there are enough mixers for nonalcoholic drinks. A late-afternoon or early-evening party will see an increased demand for white wine and mild mixed drinks, while the traditional party (8 P.M. onward) will see the greatest quantity and diversity of drinks consumed. If the party is in recognition of an anniversary, special event or holiday, guests will drink accordingly. For instance, champagne or sparkling wine will be popular on anniversaries and New Year's Eve, just as eggnog and punch is in order for a Christmas party. If you can accommodate everyone's choice of drink, the party will benefit greatly. This section will help you make your bar a success at every party.

LIQUOR

If the drinking preferences of your guests are very eccentric, you may have to pick up some special ingredients. If your guests' tastes are typical, you should be adequately covered by the Basic Bar list in Appendix 3, and will definitely be covered by the Solid Bar list. The first thing you need to do when preparing for a party is check liquor quantities on hand. Unless you want to go to the liquor store during a party, it may behoove you to purchase extra bottles of those liquors which will be most popular. Vodka is by far the most popular liquor, followed by gin. The reason vodka and gin are so popular is that they are both neutral grain spirits and therefore combine very well with any mixer. Following the neutral grain spirits in popularity are rum, whiskey, Scotch, and brandy. If you plan to purchase extra bottles of liquor, patronize a liquor store which will accept returns of unopened bottles. Always check with the liquor store at the time of purchase regarding its return policy.

There can be a wide variation in the amount of wine you will serve, depending on the nature of the party. If you are having a dinner party, plan on serving quite a lot of white and red wine. It is important to know a little bit about the difference between red and white wine. Though white wine is far more popular (approximately five times more popular) than red wine, white wine drinkers tend to be (at least in this bartender's experience) less finicky with regards to taste. The red wine drinker on average has a more discriminating taste than his or her white wine counterpart. For this reason, you can probably get by with two different white wines, while you may want to purchase several varieties of red to assure that your guests are well cared for. White wine should be served chilled and therefore kept in the refrigerator or only partially packed in ice (so as not to make the wine too cold) prior to serving (45 to 50 degrees). Reds are served at or just below room temperature. Lighter reds and rosés are served with a slight chill (55 to 65 degrees). Champagne or sparkling wine should be served cold; the temperature will act as a catalyst in forming bubbles (39 to 45 degrees). A rule of thumb for serving wine, especially at dinner parties, is that light wines (whites) should be served prior to heavier wines (reds). The old rule that white wine should be served with fish and poultry and red wine with meat is still followed, but not as strictly as in the past.

BEER

If you are having a party of fifteen or more guests, expect at least a few cases of beer to be consumed. A case or two of beer can take up a great deal of refrigerator space, so unless you have plenty of cold storage space, you will be faced with a dilemma. Kegs may or may not be the answer to this problem. A keg (technically a half barrel) is equal to approximately seven cases, while a quarter barrel (half keg) is equal to approximately three and a half cases. Though they do not take up much cold storage (they can be placed in garbage cans filled with ice), kegs may be too informal for some parties, unless a bartender is pouring the beer for the guests. Another factor not to be overlooked is that today there are many distinct taste preferences. Some people drink only light beer, others prefer premium beers such as micro-brewed or imported, and still others drink nonalcoholic. Unless the party is very large, a keg of each may be overkill. You may opt for a keg, or quarter barrel, of regular domestic beer or light beer, and cases of premium or imported beer. You should also plan to purchase nonalcoholic beer.

Beer creates a situation which requires some preparty thought, so you should make some estimates of who drinks what type of beer and how much of it. You should also figure out how much cold storage space will be available for beer at party time, remembering that there will be other items (like party food) vying for that same space. If you decide to purchase cases of beer, it's important to remember that you might need to go out for more cold beer. If you've consumed any alcohol, it's probably unwise to drive to the liquor store. You should either abstain from drinking the night of your party, ask a friend who abstains to drive you to the liquor store, or find a liquor store which will deliver in a timely fashion.

SHOTS, SHOOTERS, OR MIXED SHOTS

Depending on the theme of the party, mixed shots can be a lot of fun. Whether or not you will be able to make shots during the party will depend on your preparty planning, how efficiently you tend bar, and how busy you will be during the party. Just like bartenders who work in busy nightclubs, the most popular shots can be made prior to your night's duties.

To make a bottle of shots, simply fill a bottle (liquor bottles look the best, but any bottle will do) with the proper proportions of each ingredient of the given shot. Then place the bottle in a refrigerator until the party begins, at which time you can bury the bottle in ice, and serve to those who are interested. Two shots that are frequently premixed are Watermelons and Kamikazes. The recipe for either has equal parts of three ingredients, so fill the bottle a third with each ingredient. As with all premixed shots, unless your mix is way off, you will not be able to taste the difference. This is because a shot is small and consumed quickly. If you or those you are entertaining enjoy stronger shots, popular chilled shots are sambuca, Jägermeister, and Rumple Minze (peppermint schnapps). These bottles can be refrigerated, or chilled in a shaker with ice just prior to serving.

MIXERS

At a home party, mixers are a major component of the bar, which should create no problem. They will not hog the refrigerator or cooler during a party. If just for an evening, with the exception of milk, all mixers including juice can be kept at room temperature. When compiling a list of your guests' drinking preferences use the list not only for alcohol but the necessary mixers as well. Keep in mind some of your guests may be drinking mixers exclusively, most notably cola, diet cola, and lemon-lime soda (7-Up or Sprite). Those drinking these soft drinks will consume a greater quantity of them, so purchase accordingly.

GARNISHES

You will need fresh limes and lemons for your party. Other garnishes, including oranges, Maraschino cherries, and celery stalks, are optional. Limes are your most important garnish, and you should plan on approximately one lime for every ten guests. You should be able to get by with one lemon for about every fifty guests. Just prior to the party you should cut the fruit (refer to the section on cutting and serving garnishes, page 24). After cutting, keep the various garnishes in separate bowls in the refrigerator until you begin serving drinks, at which time they can be kept at room temperature on the bar for the remainder of the party.

GLASSES

Having enough glasses for your party is of paramount importance. For a four-hour party you should plan on at least two to three glasses per person; if you are using plastic cups, four or five per person should suffice. If you are having a very large party, you may either want to rent glasses or use plastic cups. Your decision should be based on the formality of the evening as well as your ability, if you choose glasses, to clean and recycle them. Using plastic cups is acceptable, but being short of glasses or cups is not.

The most important glasses for a party are rocks glasses, both large and small. Though not entirely appropriate for serving wine or hot drinks, rocks glasses can accommodate most any other drink, even straight-up drinks or shots if necessary.

To add a special touch to smaller parties you may want to chill glasses. Chilling glasses is easily accomplished by placing the glasses in the refrigerator or freezer prior to the party. Placed in the refrigerator, glasses should be sufficiently chilled in a couple of hours, while the freezer should do the job in less than half an hour. If you enjoy a deep frost on your glasses, run some water over the glass before putting it in the freezer. If you have not chilled any glasses prior to the party, refer to the pointers in Appendix 1 ("Serving") as a simple and quick way to chill any glass quickly.

ICE

Ice is as important as any other component of your bar. It is imperative that you have enough ice. If you make your mixed drinks correctly, you will be using quite a lot of ice, so you shouldn't worry about going overboard. A rule of thumb for a four-hour party is approximately one pound of ice per person and, as might be expected, a little more in the summer and less in the winter.

Finding a container to hold ice for drinks during the party should not be a problem. If your bar setup has a sink with two basins or tubs, using one of these tubs to store ice is your best option, otherwise a large ice bucket or a cooler will suffice. The party's back-up ice can be kept in your freezer, in a neighbor's freezer, or outside if it is cold enough.

FOOD

Don't forget food when planning for your party. Whether your food selection is as simple as chips and dip or as extensive as a catered buffet table, food is a necessity for most any party.

THE BAR SETUP

A makeshift bar can be anything from a kitchen counter to a card table or anything else with space for the bar's items at about waist height. You will want to set up all of the necessary bar supplies in an orderly and efficient manner. Add a touch of class to your bar setup by setting everything atop an attractive tablecloth. There are a few other items you should not forget. You will need a bar towel for any spills, and if you allow smoking, an ashtray is a must. Dry and wet trash receptacles will allow you to keep efficient control of the party's waste. If you mix liquid and solid waste in one trash receptacle the solid waste will cover the heavier liquid waste and you will not be able to gauge when the bag reaches its maximum weight capacity.

BARTENDING THE PARTY

Though this book is geared toward teaching you how to tend bar, there are times when doing so would be detrimental to your party. Who should tend bar depends on several factors. The first factor to take into account is the number of people you expect. If the party is indoors and you expect at least thirty guests, you should consider hiring a bartender. If the party is expected to serve a contingent of fifty or more guests, a professional bartender is a must. For indoor parties of over a hundred people, two professional bartenders are in order. The second factor to take into account when deciding who will tend the bar is the formality of the occasion. Formal parties require a professional bartender, more casual affairs leave a great deal of leeway to the host. An informal outdoor party, even a large one, may allow you to leave the bartending to your guests. A large table with all the necessary components of a bar should be sufficient and appropriate for this type of occasion. If you are thinking of bartending for your own party, before doing so you should also take into account how much time this will allow for you to interact with your guests.

INDEX